Self-Love, Self-Confidence, and Self-Esteem for Teen Girls 101

SEVEN EFFECTIVE TOOLS TO OVERCOME INSECURITIES, CONQUER FEAR, AND EMBRACE MINDFULNESS TO BUILD A POSITIVE SELF-IMAGE

LIZANNE DOUGLAS

Contents

BONUS
Self
Love
Self
Confidence
& Self
Esteem
for
Teen Girls
SCAN ME FOR
PAPER COPY ON
AMAZON
Mindful Coloring Activities,
Positive Mantras and
Daily Planner
SCAN ME FREE FOR
DIGITAL COPY
LIZANNE DOUGLAS

Introduction

Imagine walking into a high school cafeteria, where everyone seems to have found their clique, their comfort zone, laughing and sharing stories. Over in the corner, there's Emily, a fifteen-year-old who usually keeps to herself, doodling in her sketchpad. She's funny and smart, but if you asked her, she wouldn't say that about herself. Instead, she often feels like she doesn't quite fit in, questioning if she's smart enough, attractive enough, or good enough at all.

If you've picked up this book, maybe you feel a bit like Emily. Maybe you scroll through your social media feeds and feel like you're just not measuring up to the glossy lives you see there. Maybe those feelings dig deep, making you doubt your worth and the unique stuff about you that's really cool.

You're not alone in this. That's actually why this book exists. It's here because you might be looking for some real talk on how to deal with the tough stuff—like not feeling good enough for your friends, for your school, or even for yourself. This book is about finding a way to be okay with who you are right now and getting to a place where you can genuinely feel good about yourself. It's about moving away from those harsh self-judgments and learning to appreciate your own value.

As a mother of five girls, two teens, fifteen and thirteen (being in my life from ages nine and ten), one preteen (eleven years old), an eight-year-old, and a four-year-old, I've been personally involved in their life challenges. Each one of them is unique, with different looks, personalities, strengths, and weaknesses. Plus, having been a teen myself, I understand the complex emotions and experiences they will face.

This book is more than just a good read; it is a powerful, life-changing guide to a more confident and fulfilled you. The S.E.L.F.I.E. approach, outlined in each chapter, introduces practical tools that are specifically designed to improve your self-awareness, emotional intelligence, and personal growth. Here's a brief look at these empowering tools:

1. Self-Awareness: Embracing Your Unique Self

Start your journey by building a foundation of self-awareness. This tool helps you discover and affirm who you really are, boosting your confidence by aligning your self-perception with your true potential.

2. Emotion Regulation: Growing through What You Go Through

Learn to effectively manage and regulate your emotions to enhance your resilience. This skill allows you to navigate through life's ups and downs with grace and composure.

3. Love: Loving Yourself Unconditionally

Develop a nurturing and forgiving relationship with yourself.

Practice self-compassion and mindfulness to appreciate your intrinsic worth without conditions.

4. Love: Building Healthy Relationships and Letting Go of Toxic People

Focus on cultivating positive relationships that enrich your life and recognize when to distance yourself from harmful connections.

5. Flaws: Conquering Perfectionism

Embrace your imperfections and understand that they are a part of what makes you unique. This tool encourages you to let go of unrealistic expectations and be more accepting of yourself.

6. Integrity: Staying True to Yourself

Strengthen your personal integrity by learning to uphold your values and beliefs, even when faced with external pressures. This empowers you to live authentically and maintain your self-respect.

7. Enrichment: Cultivating a Growth Mindset

Adopt a mindset that views challenges as opportunities for growth. This perspective motivates continuous personal development and the pursuit of your ambitions.

The dual tools under "Love" in Chapters 3 and 4 emphasize the importance of internal and external harmony in personal development. Together, these chapters guide you on how to cherish yourself and foster healthy interpersonal dynamics.

By integrating the S.E.L.F.I.E. tools into your daily life, you'll not only enhance your understanding of yourself but also improve your interactions with the world around you. Equip yourself with these strategies to navigate your teenage years with confidence and emerge empowered to face the future.

Celebrities like Emma Watson, Billie Eilish, and Justin Bieber have been super open about their struggles with feeling insecure. They've shared their stories about overcoming self-doubt and growing into their confidence. They, just like many of us, have had to find ways to believe in themselves despite the pressures they face. This book is packed with advice that can help you do just that. It's about using what you learn here to start seeing yourself in a better light. You'll get practical steps to help you build up your self-esteem, cut down on comparisons with others, and start recognizing your own strengths.

Imagine getting up each morning and actually feeling good as you get ready for your day. Think about how it would feel to look in the mirror and actually like what you see—not just your face or your outfit but the real you looking back. That's what you're working toward. This book is going to show you how to get there by helping you understand yourself better, appreciate your own qualities, and build up the confidence that sticks around, even on tough days.

We'll tackle why feeling bad about yourself is more than just having a rough day and how you can turn things around. You'll learn how to make choices that are right for you, set goals that make you want to jump out of bed in the morning, and create a life where you feel like you belong. This book is exactly what you need right now, and it's all about helping you make real, authentic changes. It's going to be a guide, a friend, and a new way to look at everything you are—and everything you can be.

Welcome to a new beginning—one where you learn to love being you. Let's get started. As you progress through the pages, you will encounter various exercises and reflections designed to deepen your understanding of who you are and how you can cultivate a stronger, more positive self-image. These activities are not just theoretical but are based on proven psychological principles that have helped countless individuals redefine their self-perception and lead more fulfilling lives.

Additionally, this book addresses the common pitfalls and traps that exacerbate feelings of low self-worth, such as the perpetual cycle of social media comparison and the pressure to meet unrealistic standards. You will learn how to navigate these challenges with practical tips on managing your digital footprint and setting realistic personal expectations.

Furthermore, the book will guide you through transforming your social media experience into a positive one. Instead of being a source of insecurity, your online platforms can become spaces of inspiration and self-expression. You can follow people who motivate you, share parts of your journey, and connect with a community that supports and uplifts you. By curating what you see and engage with, you turn social media from a battleground of comparisons into a source of positive energy and affirmation.

You'll also discover the importance of setting boundaries, not only online but in your personal life as well. Learning to say no to things that drain you and yes to things that fulfill you is a critical skill that will be covered in detail. This empowerment extends to forming healthier relationships and taking control of your mental and emotional space.

This book is your first step toward a brighter, more confident future. By the end, you'll not only feel better equipped to handle the pressures of teenage life, but you'll also have a clearer understanding of your personal worth and how to uphold it in all aspects of life. This is your moment to shine, to show the world the real you without fear or hesitation. Join me as we embark on this transformative journey together.

S-Self-awareness
E
E
I
L
F

CHAPTER 1

S—Self-Awareness—Embracing Your Unique Self—Building Confidence Based on Who You Really Are

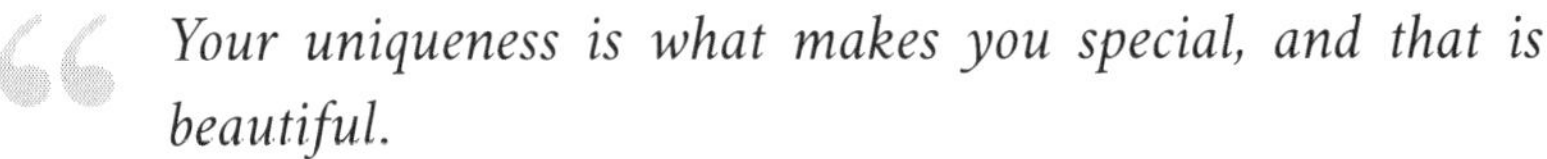

> *Your uniqueness is what makes you special, and that is beautiful.*
>
> — NIA JAX

Do you ever feel like you don't measure up? As you scroll through your social media feed, checking out one perfect picture after the next, everyone seems happier, prettier, and more confident than you. Then you look at all the "likes" and followers those "perfect people" have. Yours doesn't come close. It's like they're living in a world you only get to visit through your screen.

Sound familiar? If so, you're not alone. A survey covering over 17,500 girls, just like you, found that while nearly 68 percent felt confident back in 2017, that number has dropped to just 55 percent today. Why? Well, as our time spent online goes up, it seems our confidence takes a dive.

Here's something that might not surprise you: Studies tell us that girls often feel less confident than boys. Girls can be brutal critics of themselves and others. Many are obsessed with how they look, how they dress, and how many friends (and followers) they have. But why is that?

Boys are competitive, that's for sure. The difference is, however, that they typically compete in physical, outward ways like sports, while girls tend to be more emotionally based, competing on a different level.

Studies also show that boys spend less time on social media than girls do. Could this be why they seem less affected by the pressures of social media? Perhaps it's because they engage with it differently, focusing more on activities and competition rather than appearance and social validation.

Understanding this difference helps us see that our self-worth should not hinge on digital feedback or comparisons. Don't worry. I'm not suggesting you ditch social media. It's a powerful tool for connection and creativity, and, let's be honest, it can be really fun. Instead, think about how you can use it wisely. Remember, social media is a highlight reel, not the full story. Everyone has ups and downs, but most people only share their best moments. Keep this in mind when you find yourself comparing your everyday life to someone else's polished posts.

Take a step back, focus on what makes you unique, and use your platforms to express the real you—not just what you think others want to see. This approach might not only change how you view social media but also how you see yourself. It can help you develop a sense of self that is grounded in real, not virtual, achievements and qualities.

SELF-ESTEEM

What Is Self-Esteem?

When we talk about self-esteem, we often think about how we feel when we look in the mirror or what we believe about ourselves when we succeed or fail at something. But self-esteem isn't just about feeling good or bad about yourself—it actually influences many important areas of your life. Let's break down how a healthy (or unhealthy) sense of self-worth can affect everything, from your choices to your relationships.

Decision-Making Process

Your level of self-esteem strongly influences how you make decisions. With high self-esteem, you're more likely to trust your judgment and make choices that align with your values and goals. You feel confident enough to take calculated risks and step out of your comfort zone when necessary. On the other hand, if you struggle with low self-esteem, you might find it harder to make decisions because you doubt your abilities and fear failure. This can lead to missed opportunities and feelings of regret or frustration.

Relationships

Self-esteem shapes how you interact with others. When you value yourself, you're more likely to seek out and cultivate relationships that are respectful and supportive. High self-esteem allows you to set healthy boundaries and assert your needs effectively, which are key for maintaining fulfilling connections with friends, family, and romantic partners. Conversely, if your self-esteem is low, you might tolerate negative or toxic behavior from others because you don't believe you deserve better, which can lead to unhealthy relationships.

Emotional Health

How you feel about yourself directly impacts your emotional health. High self-esteem is associated with positive emotions like happiness, resilience, and a sense of fulfillment. If you're confident in who you are, you're better equipped to handle stress and recover from setbacks. Low self-esteem, however, can lead to feelings of worthlessness, depression, and anxiety. It can make you more vulnerable to mental health challenges because negative thoughts about yourself can spiral and become overwhelming.

Overall Well-Being

Your overall well-being is the sum of how you think, feel, and interact with the world—and self-esteem plays a huge role in this. With a healthy level of self-esteem, you're more likely to take care of your physical and mental health. You might engage in activities that promote wellness, like exercising, eating well, and seeking help when you need it. People with low self-esteem often neglect their health, which can lead to problems like chronic stress, fatigue, and a host of other health issues.

Motivation

Lastly, self-esteem can either fuel or extinguish your motivation. When you believe in yourself, you're driven to pursue goals and challenges because you see yourself as capable and worthy of achieving great things. This positive outlook fosters perseverance, which is crucial for accomplishing any long-term goal. However, if you have low self-esteem, you might struggle to find the motivation to try because you don't see the point in putting effort into something you believe you'll fail at or don't deserve.

Understanding these aspects of self-esteem can help you realize just how big of a role your sense of self-worth plays in your daily life. By working on building and maintaining a healthy self-esteem, you empower yourself to live more fully and face life's challenges with confidence. This section of our book is about starting that journey, taking steps to recognize your value, and learning to see yourself through a lens of self-respect and appreciation.

PRIMARY REASONS TEENS HAVE LOW SELF-ESTEEM

What's really behind low self-esteem in teens? It turns out that there's a lot. Let's break down some of the main points:

Social Media and Phone Use: Self-Esteem in the Digital Age

It's super common for teens to feel pressure from constant exposure to glamorized images and lifestyles on platforms like Instagram and Snapchat. A study showed that this pressure isn't all in your head. Researchers found that the more you engage in social comparison—like checking out how you stack up against others—the more you might start feeling down about yourself.

This can lead to an endless cycle of checking, comparing, feeling worse, and then checking again, especially if you're not feeling great about your looks or your life at the moment.

Peer Pressure and Social Situations

Hanging out with friends can be great, but it can also be a source of stress. Whether it's about fitting in with a certain group, feeling pressure to do things you're not comfortable with, or just trying to navigate the complex social dynamics of high school, peer influence is huge. It can make you doubt yourself and force you into a mold that doesn't really fit. This kind of pressure can chip away at your self-confidence because you're constantly trying to meet others' expectations instead of focusing on your own values and interests.

Body Image

How you feel about your body can seriously affect your self-esteem. If you find yourself often comparing your appearance to others or to unrealistic beauty standards shown in the media, it can lead to a lot of negative feelings. This is especially true if you think you don't measure up. Remember, everyone's body is different, and that diversity is what makes humans pretty cool. Trying to fit into a narrow idea of beauty just isn't realistic or healthy.

Depression and Anxiety

Mental health issues like depression and anxiety can take a big toll on how you feel about yourself. They can make everything feel harder and make you doubt your worth and abilities. It's like trying to run a race with a heavy backpack. These feelings are tough to carry, and without the right support, they can make everything else in life feel less colorful and more challenging.

Parent Influence

The way your parents or guardians see you and treat you can really shape your self-esteem. If you're constantly getting criticized or if you don't feel supported at home, it can make you feel like you're not good enough. But on the flip side, feeling loved and accepted as you are can boost your confidence massively.

Dealing with low self-esteem isn't just about changing how you feel about yourself. It's about understanding where these feelings come from and addressing them. Whether that means taking a break from social media, talking to someone about your mental health, or standing up for yourself in social situations, remember, you're not alone in this, and there are ways to feel better.

SIGNS OF LOW SELF-ESTEEM

Recognizing low self-esteem can be tricky, especially since it doesn't always look the same in everyone. Here's an exploration of some common signs that might indicate a struggle with self-esteem, particularly in teens like you:

Avoiding Tasks or Challenges

Ever felt like not even trying something because you're sure you'll fail? That's a classic sign of low self-esteem. This avoidance can be about not wanting to tackle challenges because you fear that failure might confirm your worst fears about yourself.

Quitting

Starting a new project, game, or hobby but giving up almost immediately is another red flag. It often happens because the fear of not performing well becomes overwhelming or because there's a lack of belief in one's own abilities to succeed.

Cheating or Lying

Sometimes, the pressure to succeed or to meet others' expectations becomes so intense that cheating or lying seems like the only option. This can be about wanting to avoid judgment or criticism, reflecting doubts about one's own ability to achieve success honestly.

Showing Signs of Regression

Regression means reverting to behaviors that are typical of an earlier stage of development. For example, a teenager might start to throw tantrums like a much younger child when things don't go their way, signaling a struggle with coping in a more mature manner.

Being Controlling, Bossy, or Inflexible

When you feel out of control internally, trying to control everything externally can feel like a way to compensate. Being overly bossy or inflexible can be a defense mechanism to hide feelings of insecurity or inadequacy.

Making Excuses

Frequent excuses can be a sign of low self-esteem, especially if they're used to avoid trying new things or taking on challenges. It's often easier to find a reason not to do something than to face the possibility of failing.

Falling Grades

A sudden drop in academic performance can be linked to low self-esteem, especially if the decline is not related to a lack of understanding or ability. It might be more about a lack of belief in one's capabilities or a fear of trying and not living up to expectations.

Withdrawing Socially

Pulling back from friends and activities can be a major sign of low self-esteem. It might feel safer to avoid social situations altogether than to risk judgment or rejection from peers.

Experiencing Changing Moods

Rapid and frequent changes in mood can be a symptom of internal turmoil caused by low self-esteem. Feeling great one moment and terrible the next can be confusing and exhausting, and it often stems from an unstable self-image.

Making Self-Critical Comments

If you often hear yourself or others making harshly critical statements about themselves, it's likely a sign of low self-esteem. Phrases like "I'm so stupid" or "I can never do anything right" are clues.

Being Overly Concerned or Sensitive

High sensitivity to criticism or a preoccupation with what others think can be indicative of low self-esteem. This can lead to a lot of anxiety about how one is perceived and an inability to shrug off even mild criticism.

Being Easily Influenced by Peers

When you're not feeling great about yourself, it's easier for peers to sway your opinions or decisions. This susceptibility can lead to changing your behavior just to fit in or avoid conflict, even if it goes against your personal values.

Having a Hard Time with Practically EVERYTHING

This vague sign often shows up as trouble getting things done, whether it's schoolwork, chores, or following through on commitments. It may be due to a lack of belief in one's own efficacy or ability to complete tasks. Remember, if you think you can, you are right. You can. If you think you can't, well ... unfortunately, you are usually right as well.

Recognizing these signs in yourself or others isn't about labeling someone; it's about understanding underlying issues and finding ways to address them. Self-esteem is fluid and can change with time and effort, and recognizing these signs is the first step toward building a stronger, more resilient sense of self.

EFFECTS OF LOW SELF-ESTEEM DURING TEENAGE YEARS

Low self-esteem during the teenage years doesn't just affect how you feel about yourself in the moment; it can have long-reaching consequences that stretch into adulthood.

Signs You Might Be Struggling

So, how can you tell if low self-esteem is affecting you? Keep an eye out for these signals:

- **Poor Health Choices**: Teens with low self-esteem often engage in risky behaviors, like substance abuse or unsafe sex, which can lead to serious health issues later in life.
- **Criminal Behavior:** A lack of self-worth can sometimes push individuals toward criminal activities as a way to gain approval or assert control.
- **Economic Limitations**: Low self-esteem can affect academic and job performance, limiting career opportunities and economic potential.
- **Relationship Problems**: Struggling with self-esteem can make it difficult to form and maintain healthy relationships, leading to social isolation and persistent loneliness.
- **Mental Health Issues:** Prolonged low self-esteem can contribute to long-term mental health problems, including depression, anxiety, and severe stress.

Recognizing these potential effects can be a powerful motivator for addressing and improving self-esteem during these critical years.

How It Plays Out

Low self-esteem can mess with more than just your mood; it can affect your schoolwork and your relationships. If you're not feeling great about yourself, you might not put your hand up in class or go for opportunities like leadership roles, which can affect your grades and future plans. Relationship-wise, not feeling top-notch can make it hard to form close bonds because you might not think you're worth someone else's time or affection.

Feeling constantly down about yourself can also make you more prone to feeling anxious or sad. It's really hard to keep your head up when, inside, you feel like you're not measuring up. Hang on, though. You don't have to stay down in the dumps. It's never too late to turn things around.

STEPS TO BOOST YOUR SELF-ESTEEM

Building up your self-esteem might sound like a huge task, but it's totally doable with small, everyday actions. Setting achievable goals, spending time with people who lift you up, and actively countering negative thoughts about yourself are all steps in the right direction.

Remember, it's totally normal and okay to ask for help if you're feeling stuck. Sometimes, chatting with a counselor or therapist can give you tools and ideas for boosting your self-worth that you hadn't thought of before.

Improving your self-esteem isn't just about feeling better now—it's about setting yourself up for a happier, healthier future. You deserve to recognize just how awesome you really are.

High Self-Esteem Looks Like

On the flip side, if your self-esteem is healthy, you're likely to:

- Feel confident enough to try new things and seize opportunities.
- Handle setbacks calmly because you know you can cope with them.
- Take pride in your achievements, whether big or small.
- Help others, knowing you have something valuable to contribute.
- Self-esteem isn't just a fancy term—it's a real force in your life that affects how you think, feel, and act.

Remember, the way you view yourself affects so many aspects of your life, but it's something you can change. It starts by recognizing your own strengths and giving yourself credit for them. You're capable of more than you think!

SELF-CONFIDENCE

What Is Self-Confidence?

In the journey to understand and improve yourself, self-awareness is your best tool. Before you can start building up your self-esteem and self-confidence, you first need to really get to know who you are, what you feel, and why you act the way you do. Let's get deeper into understanding the meanings of self-confidence and self-esteem, exploring which comes first, and uncovering the concept of false self-esteem.

Self-Confidence vs. Self-Esteem: Understanding the Difference

Although they might sound similar, self-confidence and self-esteem are not the same thing. Self-confidence is about your trust in your ability to perform tasks, make decisions, and face new challenges. It's knowing that you can ace a test, give a killer presentation, or learn a new skill. Self-confidence is often specific to the situation or task at hand and can vary greatly depending on what you're doing.

Self-esteem, on the other hand, is about how much you value yourself and how worthy you believe you are of happiness, respect, and love. It's a deeper and more stable sense of personal value that isn't as dependent on external achievements or failures. High self-esteem means you generally think you're a good person who deserves good things in life, regardless of how well you can shoot a basketball or solve math problems.

Which Comes First: Self-Esteem or Self-Confidence?

It's like the chicken and the egg situation. Many people wonder which should come first: self-esteem or self-confidence. The truth is they build on each other. Typically, having a solid base of self-esteem can make it easier to develop self-confidence. When you value yourself and feel secure in who you are, you're more likely to take on challenges and believe in your abilities to succeed in specific tasks. Conversely, each time you succeed at something, your self-esteem gets a boost because you feel more capable and accomplished, reinforcing your overall sense of worth.

Can You Have Confidence but Low Self-Esteem?

Yes, it's possible to have self-confidence in certain areas while still having low self-esteem. For example, someone might be very confident in their academic abilities or sports skills but still feel unworthy of love or happiness. They might think, "Sure, I'm good at math, but that doesn't make me a lovable person." This scenario is common and can be quite confusing. It shows why it's important to work on both self-confidence and self-esteem as separate but interconnected parts of your self-awareness.

What Is False Self-Esteem?

False self-esteem is when someone appears to have high self-esteem because they boast, brag, or show off, but deep down, they don't truly believe in their own self-worth. It's like a mask of confidence people wear to cover up their insecurities. They might constantly seek attention or approval from others to feel good about themselves, or they might get defensive and angry if someone criticizes them. This behavior is a shield to protect against feelings of inadequacy or unworthiness that lurk beneath the surface.

Building Genuine Self-Esteem and Self-Confidence

Now that we understand the differences and how these aspects of self can intersect, how do you start building genuine self-esteem and self-confidence? Here are a few strategies:

- **Reflection**: Spend time getting to know yourself. What are your strengths and weaknesses? What makes you feel good? Reflecting on these questions can help you understand where your self-esteem and self-confidence levels are at.

- **Set Achievable Goals**: Start small and set goals that are achievable but still challenging. Each success will build your confidence, and each effort will reinforce your self-esteem.
- **Practice Self-Compassion**: Be kind to yourself. Everyone makes mistakes, and no one is perfect. Learning to be compassionate toward yourself helps foster genuine self-esteem.
- **Seek Feedback**: Constructive feedback, not just praise, can help you understand and appreciate your real capabilities and worth. It also helps identify areas for improvement, making your self-confidence more resilient.
- **Affirmations and Positive Self-Talk:** Remind yourself of your worth and abilities. Positive self-talk can reinforce what you feel about yourself and help turn fleeting confidence into a stable sense of self-esteem.
- **Therapy or Counseling**: Sometimes, talking to a professional can help untangle the feelings and behaviors that cloud your self-perception. This can be especially helpful if you're struggling with false self-esteem or if there's a significant gap between your self-esteem and self-confidence.

CONFIDENCE: WHY IT'S IMPORTANT

Understanding and developing self-awareness, self-esteem, and self-confidence can seem like a lot, but it's a journey worth taking. By focusing on these elements, you set yourself up for a more fulfilling and successful life, where you not only achieve great things but also truly appreciate and love yourself for who you are.

Self-confidence is not just about feeling good; it's a foundational quality that affects virtually every aspect of your life. From how you handle stress and challenges to how you interact with others, self-confidence plays a pivotal role. Let's explore in detail why building self-confidence is crucial for your overall well-being and success.

Less Fear and Anxiety

One of the most immediate benefits of self-confidence is experiencing less fear and anxiety in everyday situations. When you're confident in your abilities, you're less likely to feel nervous about upcoming events or challenges. This is because self-confidence reduces the uncertainty that typically fuels anxiety. For instance, if you're confident in your public speaking skills, you're less likely to dread a class presentation; you know you can handle it. This decrease in fear and anxiety makes it easier for you to step out of your comfort zone and try new things, leading to personal growth and opportunities.

Greater Motivation

Self-confidence also directly impacts your motivation levels. When you believe in your capabilities, you're more likely to pursue your goals with enthusiasm and persistence. This is because self-confidence helps you visualize success, which is a powerful motivator. It transforms challenges into something you look forward to conquering rather than obstacles that might trip you up. For example, if you're confident in your ability to solve complex math problems, you'll be more motivated to take advanced classes and engage with difficult material, seeing it as an opportunity to improve and learn rather than a potential failure.

More Resilience

As mentioned, resilience is your ability to bounce back from setbacks and failures. Self-confidence is key here because it gives you a foundational belief in your own strengths and abilities, which helps you recover from disappointments. Confident individuals see failures as temporary and specific learning opportunities rather than reflections of their inherent worth or potential. This perspective allows them to maintain their morale and continue working toward their goals even when things don't go as planned.

Improved Relationships

Confidence can significantly enhance your relationships. When you feel good about yourself, you're more likely to enter into interactions with positive energy and open communication. You're less likely to project insecurities onto others or build relationships based on neediness or dependency. Additionally, confident people are generally seen as more attractive and reliable partners, friends, and colleagues because they emit a sense of stability and strength. They are also better at setting and respecting boundaries, which is crucial for healthy relationships.

Stronger Sense of Your Authentic Self

Finally, self-confidence is deeply tied to a strong sense of your authentic self. When you're confident, you're more in tune with your values, desires, and passions. You're less likely to conform to others' expectations or societal pressures, which allows you to live a life that truly reflects who you are. This authenticity brings a sense of fulfillment and happiness that is hard to achieve when you don't feel confident in who you are. It encourages you to follow your own path and make choices that align with your true self, not just the self you think you're supposed to be.

Building a Foundation of Confidence

Developing self-confidence is a dynamic and ongoing process. It involves consistently challenging yourself, celebrating small victories, learning from your experiences, and affirming your worth. Remember, self-confidence isn't about never feeling doubts—it's about not letting those doubts stop you from moving forward.

Whether you're working on reducing your anxiety, boosting your motivation, fostering resilience, improving your relationships, or embracing your authenticity, increasing your self-confidence can be the key to unlocking your full potential. As you grow more confident, you'll find that many areas of your life improve alongside it. It's about more than just feeling sure of yourself; it's about creating a life where you can thrive.

SELF-AWARENESS: WHERE IT ALL BEGINS

As we've explored the importance of self-esteem and self-confidence, it's clear that both are deeply influenced by how well you know and understand yourself. This understanding begins with self-awareness, which is the foundation upon which you can start to improve these aspects of your life. For teens, especially in an age dominated by social media, achieving self-awareness can be both challenging and incredibly rewarding.

What Is Self-Awareness?

Self-awareness is knowing who you are at your core. It involves understanding your thoughts, feelings, motivations, and behaviors. It also means recognizing how your actions affect both your own mental state and that of the people around you. This might sound a bit heavy, but it's really about tuning in to what makes you tick. Having self-awareness can boost your self-confidence and self-esteem, as it helps us to truly know ourselves and our abilities.

How to Develop Self-Awareness

Developing self-awareness can seem daunting, but it can be approached in simple ways. For example, journaling your thoughts and feelings daily can help you notice patterns in your behavior. Meditation or mindfulness exercises can also increase your awareness by helping you become more attuned to your present experiences. Engaging in these practices allows you to step back and observe your reactions to certain situations rather than just going through the motions.

The Power of Knowing Your Strengths and Weaknesses

Understanding your strengths and weaknesses is a vital part of self-awareness. This doesn't just mean knowing what you're good at or what you struggle with; it's about recognizing where you can leverage your talents and where you might need to ask for help or improve. For instance, you might be great at coming up with big ideas but not so great at paying attention to details. Or maybe you're a fantastic listener but find it hard to speak up in a crowd.

Knowing these things about yourself can boost your self-confidence because it empowers you to put yourself in situations where you can shine. It also helps build self-esteem by fostering a realistic sense of self. You aren't setting yourself up for failure by tackling tasks that don't play to your strengths; instead, you're acknowledging where you excel and where you can grow.

Debunking Misconceptions about Strengths and Weaknesses

A common misconception among teens is that having weaknesses means you're flawed. This couldn't be further from the truth. Everyone has weaknesses; they are just areas where we can improve. Recognizing weaknesses is not about self-criticism; it's about self-improvement and growth. It's also vital to understand that strengths can sometimes be weaknesses in disguise. For example, being highly organized is generally seen as a strength, but it can turn into a weakness if it leads to inflexibility or an inability to adapt to unexpected changes.

Another misconception is that your strengths and weaknesses are fixed. However, with effort and perseverance, you can enhance your strengths and turn your weaknesses into new areas of competency. This dynamic view encourages a growth mindset, which is essential for fostering resilience and a positive self-image.

How Does Social Media Fit In?

In today's digital age, social media can both challenge and enhance self-awareness, as we've already discussed. On one hand, constant comparison to others can distort your self-image and dampen your self-esteem. On the other hand, social media can be a tool for self-expression and for learning about different perspectives and experiences.

To use social media to your advantage, try to be mindful of the content you read and share. Follow accounts that inspire you and reflect your interests and values rather than those that make you feel inadequate or insecure. Also, use your platforms to express your true self, not just an idealized version of who you think you should be. This authenticity can reinforce your self-awareness and help you build genuine connections with others.

Building self-awareness involves curiosity, patience, and a lot of self-reflection. For teens, navigating this path can be particularly challenging, given the pressures of social media and the rapid changes you experience during these years. However, by focusing on understanding yourself better—your motives, emotions, strengths, and weaknesses—you set the stage for enhancing your self-esteem and self-confidence. Remember, the more you know about yourself, the more empowered you will be to face whatever life throws your way.

Understanding your strengths and weaknesses is a critical step in developing self-awareness, which, in turn, boosts your self-confidence and self-esteem. For teens, this can be an especially transformative process as you navigate the complexities of growing up. Here's how you can start identifying your unique traits and use this knowledge to grow.

How to Discover Your Strengths and Weaknesses

The first step in identifying your strengths and weaknesses is reflection. Think about times you felt successful or proud. What were you doing? What skills were you using? These are likely your strengths. On the other hand, consider situations where you felt frustrated or needed more help. These might point to areas where you could improve, which are your potential weaknesses.

Feedback from others can also be invaluable. Sometimes, friends, family, or teachers can see things in us that we might not notice ourselves. Ask them what they think your strengths and weaknesses are. You might be surprised at what they say!

Another method is trying new things. Engaging in a variety of activities can expose strengths and weaknesses you never knew you had. For instance, you might find out you have a knack for public speaking after joining the debate club, or you might discover you struggle with patience when learning a new sport.

BUILDING CONFIDENCE AND SELF-ESTEEM

Building Self-Confidence

Through Mastering Experiences

Mastery experiences, where you successfully overcome an obstacle or master a skill, are incredibly effective at boosting self-confidence. Every time you achieve something, whether it's big or small, it reinforces your belief in your ability to succeed. For teens, this could be as simple as improving a grade in a challenging subject or learning to drive. The key is to set realistic goals and gradually increase the difficulty to continue growing your skills and your confidence.

Learning from Others: Vicarious Experiences and Modeling Behavior

Vicarious learning, or putting yourself in someone else's shoes, where you gain confidence by seeing others perform tasks successfully, is another great way to boost your own self-belief. This could be watching a friend nail a musical performance and thinking, "If they can do it, so can I."

Similarly, modeling behavior involves observing and imitating the actions of others. If you admire how confidently a friend or a famous personality handles challenges, try adopting some of their strategies. For example, if you notice that a classmate always asks questions confidently in class, observe their behavior and perhaps try to emulate their confidence in asking questions.

The Power of Social Persuasion

Social persuasion in building self-confidence involves getting encouragement from others that you can handle specific tasks. This encouragement can significantly enhance your belief in your capabilities. When a teacher, coach, or parent encourages you by pointing out a specific ability they believe you can excel in, it can motivate you to try harder and achieve more.

Additional Tips for Building Self-Esteem and Confidence

- **Be Kind to Yourself**: It's easy to be your own worst critic, but try to recognize and challenge these unkind thoughts. Remember, it's completely okay to make mistakes—everyone does!
- **Repeat Positive Statements:** Affirmations can reinforce your self-worth. Simple statements like "I am capable" or "I am worthy" can make a big difference in how you view yourself.
- **Avoid Comparisons**: Comparing yourself to others, especially to what you see on social media, can be a fast track to feeling bad about yourself. Remember, everyone's journey is different.
- **Look after Yourself:** Regular exercise, a balanced diet, and sufficient sleep can significantly boost your mood and self-esteem. We will delve deeper into this topic in a later chapter.

- **Focus on the Positives**: Make it a habit to reflect on what went well at the end of each day. This can help shift your focus from what you're not good at to what you excel in.
- **Spend Time with Supportive People**: Surround yourself with friends and family who uplift you and believe in your abilities.
- **Learn to Assert Yourself:** Being able to express your thoughts and feelings confidently can improve how you perceive yourself authentically.
- **Do Things You Enjoy**: Engaging in activities that make you happy can improve your mood and boost your self-esteem.
- **Fake It Till You Make It:** Sometimes, just acting confident can make you feel more confident. This doesn't mean being fake, but often, by acting confidently, you start to feel it genuinely.
- **Go for It**: Stepping out of your comfort zone and trying new things can be empowering and can greatly enhance your self-perception.

INTERACTIVE ELEMENT

As we explore the realms of self-awareness, self-confidence, and self-esteem, it's vital to actively engage in exercises that promote deeper personal understanding. To help you embark on this journey, I've created a Self-Awareness Worksheet inspired by effective practices in self-discovery. This worksheet is designed to guide you through the process of identifying your strengths, weaknesses, personal preferences, and more. Completing this worksheet will not only enhance your self-awareness but also pave the way for building self-confidence and self-esteem.

Instructions

Take your time to answer each question honestly and thoughtfully. This is not a test—there are no right or wrong answers here. The goal is to reflect on your personal experiences, feelings, and beliefs to gain a better understanding of who you are and what makes you unique.

Part 1: Discovering Your Strengths and Weaknesses

Question 1: Think about a time when you achieved something you're proud of. Describe the situation and identify the skills or qualities you used to achieve this.

____

____

____

____

____

Question 2: Reflect on a challenge you faced recently. What made it difficult? What areas do you think you could improve on based on this experience?

____

____

____

____

____

Question 3: Ask two people you trust (a friend, family member, or teacher) to describe one strength and one weakness they observe in you. Note their answers here and reflect on whether you agree with their perspectives.

____

____

____

____

____

Part 2: Understanding Your Reactions

Question 4: Describe how you typically react when you receive criticism. Do you withdraw, seek to improve, or feel defensive? Why do you think you react this way?

____

____

____

____

____

Question 5: Recall a time when you felt extremely happy. What triggered these feelings? Does this reveal anything about what is important to you?

____

____

____

____

____

Part 3: Setting Personal Goals

Question 6: What is one personal goal you would like to achieve in the next year? Based on what you have learned about your strengths and weaknesses, outline a plan on how you intend to achieve this goal. Start by writing each goal, and underneath the goal, list the steps you'll need to take in order to achieve it.

____

____

___

___

___

Part 4: Reflecting on Influences

Question 7**:** What are the top three influences on your self-esteem (these could be activities, people, or thoughts)? Describe how each one impacts your feelings about yourself.

___

___

___

___

___

Question 8: Identify a person you admire for their confidence. What specific qualities or behaviors do they exhibit that you would like to emulate?

___

___

___

Part 5: Daily Affirmations and Actions

Question 9: Write down three positive affirmations that resonate with you. How can you incorporate these into your daily routine to boost your self-esteem?

Question 10: List three actions you can take this week to step out of your comfort zone. Reflect on how these actions might help you build self-confidence.

Once you have completed this worksheet, your extended assignment is to put Part 5 into action over the next week. Keep a journal of your experiences and feelings as you complete these tasks. At the end of the week, revisit this worksheet and reflect on any changes in your perceptions or feelings about yourself.

WRAPPING IT UP

This chapter has talked in depth about the ever-important subjects of self-awareness, self-esteem, and self-confidence—each vital to understanding and enhancing how you see yourself and interact with the world. We began by exploring self-awareness, the cornerstone of personal growth. It involves a profound understanding of your thoughts, feelings, and behaviors and how these influence your interactions and personal development. Recognizing the distinction between social media perceptions and real-life experiences is vital for maintaining healthy self-perceptions and avoiding detrimental comparisons.

We then examined self-esteem, which is your overall sense of worth and value. It plays a crucial role in how you value and perceive yourself, impacting everything from your motivation and mental health to your satisfaction with life. Low self-esteem can lead to poor decision-making, unsatisfying relationships, and significant emotional distress. Conversely, high self-esteem fosters resilience, enables positive interactions, and contributes to a fulfilling life. The discussion highlighted how external influences, particularly social media, can skew perceptions of self-worth by promoting unrealistic standards.

The exploration of self-confidence focused on your belief in your ability to perform tasks and face challenges. Building self-confidence through mastery experiences, vicarious learning, modeling behavior, and social persuasion strengthens your belief in your capabilities. This belief is essential for undertaking new challenges and achieving personal goals. High self-confidence encourages a proactive and optimistic approach to life, enhancing your ability to succeed and maintain psychological resilience.

The interplay between self-awareness, self-esteem, and self-confidence was emphasized throughout the chapter. For instance, improving self-awareness can boost self-esteem by helping you understand and accept your true self. In turn, enhanced self-esteem can increase self-confidence, as you feel more deserving of success and happiness. Furthermore, self-confidence can reinforce self-awareness by encouraging you to engage in new experiences that deepen your self-understanding.

Practical strategies for developing these aspects included engaging in self-reflection to increase self-awareness, setting realistic goals to build confidence, practicing self-compassion to enhance self-esteem, and seeking feedback to foster continuous personal growth.

In conclusion, this chapter provided a comprehensive guide to recognizing and nurturing your self-awareness, self-esteem, and self-confidence. By embracing your unique qualities and continuously working on these critical areas, you equip yourself to lead a more authentic, successful, and satisfying life. The journey of personal development is ongoing, requiring persistence, resilience, and a willingness to adapt and grow. As you move forward, keep in mind that these efforts will help you not only understand yourself better but also create a life that truly reflects your values and ambitions.

S
E-
Emotional
Regulation
E
I
F
L

CHAPTER 2

E—Emotional Regulation—Regulating Your Emotions—Growing Through What You Go Through

> *It's not what happens to us, but our response to what happens to us that hurts us.*
>
> — STEPHEN COVEY

Fifteen-year-old Kaylie was ecstatic when Aiden, the cutest guy in her middle school, asked her to the dance. He was shy, so it didn't surprise her that he had Marley ask for him. She was shy, too. After getting permission from her parents to go with him, she gathered her courage and approached him in the school cafeteria to ask what time he was picking her up.

Aiden seemed confused. "Do what? Picking you up?" he asked. "I have no clue what you're talking about."

Kaylie noticed Marley and the group of girls she was sitting with were snickering. There were whispers, and soon, everyone in the cafeteria was laughing, and that's when she realized she was the victim of a horrible prank.

Kaylie burst into tears. She was embarrassed, hurt, and very, very angry. She dove into a deep depression. Months later, her parents arranged an appointment with a therapist. When Kaylie confided her feelings, she was shocked when her therapist assured her, "It's not only normal to feel that way but also healthy," she said. "There's no such thing as unhealthy emotions; it is how we respond to them that matters." Accepting her feelings helped Kaylie work through them, and it can help you, too.

THE IMPORTANCE OF ACCEPTING EMOTIONS

In life, especially during our teenage years, emotions can feel as though they're on a never-ending rollercoaster—constantly up and down and, sometimes, spiraling out of control. It's crucial to understand the importance of accepting and not suppressing these emotions. Every emotion we experience, even those we might label as "unhealthy," like sadness, anger, or fear, serves a purpose. They are signals telling us about our environment and our needs.

The term "unhealthy emotions" often misleads us to believe that it's wrong to feel certain ways. However, emotions in themselves are not unhealthy; it's the actions we take in response to those emotions that can lead to negative outcomes. For instance, feeling angry is a natural human emotion, but how we choose to express that anger can be either constructive or destructive. Learning to respond to our emotions in healthy ways is a critical skill for personal development.

WHAT IS EMOTIONAL REGULATION?

This brings us to the concept of emotional regulation, which is essentially about managing the way we react to our emotions. It doesn't mean suppressing feelings but rather understanding them and responding in a way that aligns with our values and long-term goals. Emotional regulation is crucial because it helps us handle impulses and, as research suggests, can significantly impact our self-esteem. When we manage our emotions effectively, we feel more competent and confident in handling life's challenges, which in turn boosts our self-esteem.

The link between emotional regulation and self-esteem is evident when we consider how our reactions to emotions affect our perceptions of ourselves. If we lash out in anger, we might feel guilty or ashamed afterward, which can diminish our self-esteem. Conversely, if we handle a challenging situation calmly and constructively, our self-esteem is likely to increase. This self-assurance comes from knowing we can trust ourselves to manage difficult emotions without compromising our values.

Understanding and practicing emotional regulation involves several strategies, such as:

- **Recognizing Emotions**: The first step is to become aware of what you're feeling without judgment. Acknowledge that it's okay to feel these emotions.
- **Identifying Triggers**: Understanding what triggers your emotions can help you anticipate and manage your reactions better.

- **Developing Healthy Coping Strategies**: Instead of acting on impulse, find healthy ways to deal with your emotions. This could be talking to someone, writing in a journal, or engaging in a physical activity.
- **Practicing Mindfulness:** Being present in the moment can help you gain perspective on your emotions and reduce their intensity.
- **Seeking Professional Help:** Sometimes, managing emotions on our own can be challenging, and it's perfectly okay to seek help from a counselor or therapist.

WHY IS EMOTIONAL REGULATION IMPORTANT?

Identifying and accepting emotions are crucial to your well-being, but learning how to handle or regulate your emotions is what really makes the difference. By mastering emotional regulation, you not only improve your relationship with yourself but also enhance your interactions with others. It's a vital component of mental health and overall well-being. As you learn to navigate your emotional landscape with understanding and care, you'll find that you are building a foundation of strong self-esteem that will support you throughout life.

Continuing from the previous discussion on the significance of emotional regulation, it's vital to explore some of the common challenges people face in managing their emotions effectively. Emotional dysregulation, which refers to the inability to control or regulate emotional responses, can lead to significant distress, not only for the individual experiencing it but also for those around them.

COMMON CHALLENGES TO EMOTIONAL REGULATION

Emotional regulation can be difficult due to several factors, including biological predispositions, early childhood experiences, and learned behaviors. For instance, individuals who experience high levels of stress or trauma during childhood often find it harder to regulate their emotions. They might not have had the chance to learn healthy coping mechanisms, or they may have been conditioned to respond to stress in unhealthy ways.

Furthermore, our modern lifestyle can exacerbate these challenges. The fast-paced nature of today's society can lead to constant stress and burnout, which are fertile grounds for emotional dysregulation. Social media also plays a role, as it can distort our perceptions of normalcy and increase feelings of inadequacy and anxiety.

SIGNS OF EMOTIONAL DYSREGULATION

Recognizing the signs of emotional dysregulation is the first step in addressing them. Some common symptoms include:

- **Abrupt Changes in Mood:** These are often intense and seemingly unprovoked fluctuations in feelings that can disrupt daily activities.
- **Understanding Hormones and Teen Emotions**: The teenage years are a critical time for emotional development, significantly influenced by hormonal changes. Hormones like estrogen, progesterone, and testosterone play pivotal roles in how teens' brains control emotions. These hormones can cause mood swings, which are not just about the ups and downs of daily life but are also biochemical in nature.

- **Mood Swing Triggers:** Emotional fluctuations during adolescence are largely driven by the ebb and flow of hormones. However, external factors such as stress, lack of sleep, dietary changes, and the social and academic pressures of teenage life can also trigger these mood swings. Recognizing these triggers is crucial for understanding and managing emotional responses.
- **Coping Strategies:** Managing emotional dysregulation involves several proactive strategies that can help stabilize mood swings:
- **Promoting a Healthy Lifestyle**: Encouraging regular physical activity and a balanced diet can help mitigate some of the emotional turbulence associated with hormonal changes.
- **Practicing Mindfulness and Relaxation Techniques**: Techniques such as deep breathing, meditation, and yoga can be beneficial. These practices help calm the mind and can reduce the intensity of emotional responses to stress. In Chapter 3, we'll dive deeper into mindfulness and relaxation techniques.
- **Encouraging Healthy Communication**: Open and honest communication with peers, family, and mentors can provide emotional support and lessen the feelings of isolation that often accompany mood swings. You'll learn more about healthy communication in Chapter 4.
- **Seeking Professional Help:** Sometimes, the support of a counselor or therapist can be crucial. These professionals can provide strategies and interventions that are tailored to the unique challenges that teens face.
- **Binge Eating:** Using food to cope with emotional distress can lead to cycles of binge eating, where individuals consume large quantities of food in a short period.

- **Crying Spells:** Frequent, uncontrollable crying can be a response to overwhelming feelings that an individual feels incapable of managing.
- **Emotional Outbursts:** These include sudden, extreme expressions of anger, sadness, or frustration that are disproportionate to the situation.
- **Persistent Interpersonal Conflict**: Difficulty in regulating emotions can lead to frequent misunderstandings and conflicts with others.
- **Aggression or Violent Outbursts:** These are severe forms of emotional expression that can lead to physical confrontations or verbal attacks.
- **Self-Harm**: In an attempt to manage unbearable emotional pain, individuals may resort to hurting themselves physically.
- **Substance Use Disorder**: Turning to alcohol or drugs to numb feelings or escape from emotional distress is a common sign of emotional dysregulation.
- **Poor Tolerance for Frustration:** Small irritations can seem insurmountable and may trigger disproportionate emotional responses.

EXAMPLES OF EMOTIONAL DYSREGULATION

To illustrate, consider a teenager named Emily who experiences emotional dysregulation. Emily finds it difficult to manage her frustration when she's unable to meet her own high standards, particularly at school. When she scores lower than expected on a test, she might react by yelling at her friends or withdrawing into herself for days. This inability to cope with perceived failure often leads to emotional outbursts or depression, affecting her school performance and relationships.

Similarly, a seventeen-year-old named Katie was being teased by her "friends" for being "goody-goody." Tired of the pressure, she began to drink, which spiraled her into a deep depression, adding even more problems on top of her issues.

ADDRESSING EMOTIONAL DYSREGULATION

Addressing emotional dysregulation involves several strategies:

- **Therapy:** Professional help from psychologists or therapists can be invaluable. Cognitive-behavioral therapy (CBT) and dialectical behavior therapy (DBT) are particularly effective in teaching individuals how to manage their emotions and develop healthy coping mechanisms.
- **Mindfulness and Meditation**: These practices can help individuals become more aware of their emotions and their triggers without immediately reacting to them.
- **Developing a Support Network**: Building relationships with people who understand and support you can provide a stable foundation for emotional health.
- **Healthy Lifestyle Choices**: Regular exercise, sufficient sleep, and a balanced diet can improve one's overall emotional health and resilience.
- **Learning New Coping Skills:** Educating oneself on stress management techniques and actively practicing them can help mitigate the intensity of emotional reactions.

By understanding and tackling the challenges of emotional dysregulation, individuals can improve their quality of life significantly. It's not merely about suppressing emotions but learning to engage with them constructively. This journey toward emotional maturity not only enhances personal well-being but also enriches relationships and professional success.

EMOTIONAL SKILLS AND PRACTICES TO DEVELOP

Emotional regulation is a critical skill that can greatly impact your quality of life, especially during the tumultuous teenage years. Developing these skills isn't just about managing negative emotions but also embracing a fuller range of emotional experiences with grace and understanding. Here's how you can cultivate these abilities in daily life:

Allowing Your Emotions to Exist without Judgment

The first step in emotional regulation is to allow your emotions to surface without immediate judgment. Recognize that every feeling you have is valid and serves a purpose. By accepting your emotions as they are, you open the door to understanding them more deeply instead of pushing them away or labeling them as wrong.

Exploring How You Feel

Dive deeper into your emotions by exploring them. Ask yourself why you feel a certain way and what might have triggered these feelings. This exploration is not about finding quick fixes but about understanding the nuances of your emotional landscape. It's like being a detective in your own mind, curious and open to whatever comes up.

Naming Your Emotions

Put a name to what you feel. Are you angry, or are you perhaps frustrated or disappointed? Labeling your emotions accurately helps in managing them more effectively. It reduces the overwhelming nature of intense feelings and gives you a clearer perspective on what actions might help you feel better.

Accepting Your Emotions

Acceptance is key to emotional regulation. It involves acknowledging your emotions without trying to change them. This might sound crazy, but acceptance is actually a proactive step toward emotional health. It doesn't mean resignation; it means understanding that your emotions are part of you and recognizing that they are transient.

Remember Kaylie? When she went for help, her therapist shared a very important suggestion. "Don't wish it to be different," he said. "In accepting how you feel, you will be able to work through it. If you waste your energy wishing for the impossible, you'll get stuck there." He went on to explain that her emotions were natural. Who wouldn't feel hurt, sad, and angry if they were the blunt victim of such a cruel prank? It's ok to feel however you feel. It's healthy to have emotions. What is not healthy, however, is to ignore your emotions or to get stuck in them.

Practicing Mindfulness

Mindfulness is the art of being present in the moment without judgment. While this topic will be elaborated on a little further into the book, it's worth mentioning that incorporating even basic mindfulness practices into your daily routine can significantly improve your ability to regulate your emotions.

Identifying Your Triggers

Understanding what triggers your emotional responses is crucial. Triggers can be external, like a conversation or an event, or internal, like a particular thought or memory. By identifying these triggers, you can begin to anticipate and prepare for emotional responses or work on addressing the underlying causes.

Take Ellie, a sixteen-year-old girl who found that every time she heard her parents arguing, it triggered a deep anxiety within her. She realized that this stemmed from her childhood fear of instability and change. Recognizing this pattern, Ellie began to work on coping strategies that helped her manage her anxiety during these situations. She learned grounding techniques and used music to soothe herself whenever the arguments started, slowly gaining more control over her emotional reactions. You, too, will be able to spot triggers and learn techniques to apply to help you—like grounding, which will be introduced in detail later in this book.

Practicing Self-Compassion

Be kind to yourself. Self-compassion involves treating yourself with the same kindness, concern, and support you would offer a good friend. When dealing with difficult emotions, instead of being self-critical, try to be understanding toward yourself.

Challenging Negative Self-Talk

Much of our emotional distress is perpetuated by our own negative self-talk. Start noticing when you're being overly critical of yourself and challenge these thoughts. Ask yourself if you'd speak to someone else the way you speak to yourself. Often, this perspective helps you realize that you deserve compassion from yourself as much as anyone else does.

Taking a Break before Responding

When emotions run high, taking a break before responding can prevent reactions that you might regret later. Whether it's stepping away from a heated conversation or taking a few deep breaths before replying to an email, giving yourself time to cool down can help you respond more thoughtfully.

Starting an Exercise Routine

Physical activity is a powerful tool for emotional regulation. Exercise releases endorphins, often known as feel-good hormones, which can lift your mood and help you handle stress better. Starting a routine doesn't mean you need to engage in intense workouts; even regular walks or light jogging can make a significant difference.

Seeking Professional Guidance

Sometimes, the best way to develop emotional regulation skills is with the help of a professional. Therapists and counselors are trained to guide you through the process of understanding and managing your emotions. They provide a safe space to explore your feelings and develop strategies tailored to your specific needs.

DEALING WITH YOUR THOUGHTS WHILE EXPERIENCING NEGATIVE EMOTIONS

As a teenager, the way you talk to yourself in your head plays a big role in shaping how you see yourself. If you keep beating yourself up over a bad grade or a mistake, like continuously replaying a disappointing moment, it starts to paint a gloomy picture of who you are. This constant negative self-talk can really lower your self-esteem, making you feel like you're not good at anything.

Imagine if every time you did something slightly wrong, someone told you it meant you were a failure. If you heard that enough, you might start to believe it, right? That's essentially what happens when you let negative thoughts go unchecked.

Understanding and Tackling Negative Thoughts

Some of the thought patterns you may have to deal with include:

Thinking in Extremes

It's easy to fall into the trap of black-and-white thinking. For example, if a presentation doesn't go perfectly, you might beat yourself up and think it was a complete flop. But life isn't just about perfect or terrible—there's a whole spectrum in between. Recognizing that you can have an okay day or a mostly good performance helps ease the pressure of needing to be perfect. It's about learning to be okay with "good enough," which can really take the weight off your shoulders.

Making Everything a Big Deal

Consider a moment when you said something awkward and then couldn't stop thinking about it, telling yourself, "I'm always so awkward." This is you making a mountain out of a molehill. To challenge this, keep a record of all the times things went well. Maybe you made everyone laugh last week, or you had a great conversation with a friend without any awkward silences. Reminding yourself of these positive interactions helps balance your view and shows you that one awkward moment doesn't define you.

Ignoring the Good Stuff

If you tend to overlook compliments and only focus on criticism, you might be filtering out the positive. Next time you get a compliment, really listen to it; maybe even write it down. This practice helps you remember the good parts of your day and your accomplishments, which can often be overshadowed by the negative if you're not careful.

Brushing Off Compliments

Sometimes, when people compliment you, it might feel easier to just brush it off and think they're just being nice. Instead, try to take these compliments seriously. Let them sink in, and remind yourself that there's a real reason someone said something positive about you. Allow yourself to feel good about the compliment, which can help build your self-esteem.

Assuming the Worst

Jumping to conclusions can be a major source of stress, like thinking a friend is mad at you because they haven't texted back quickly. Rather than letting your mind run wild with assumptions, take a step back and look for actual evidence. Maybe they're just busy, or their phone died. Checking the facts can help you avoid a lot of unnecessary stress.

Blowing Things out of Proportion

When something goes wrong, and you can't stop thinking about it, you're probably giving it too much importance. Try putting it into perspective by asking yourself, "What's the worst that can actually happen?" Often, you'll find that the situation isn't as catastrophic as it seems, and even if it's bad, there are ways to handle it that won't be the end of the world.

Believing Your Feelings Are Facts

It's easy to think that just because you feel stupid, it means you are stupid. But your feelings aren't always the truth. Challenge these feelings by looking for real evidence that contradicts how you feel. You'll often find that your capabilities are much greater than your insecurities suggest.

Setting Unrealistic Expectations

Telling yourself you "should" be able to do something perfectly can set you up for disappointment. Instead of saying, "I should never make mistakes," try thinking, "It's okay to make mistakes sometimes." This helps you approach tasks with a more relaxed and open attitude, which can actually improve your performance.

Sticking Labels

Calling yourself names like "loser" or "hopeless" because of one mistake is an extreme reaction. Instead, focus on what exactly went wrong and how you can improve next time. Try calling yourself an "overcomer" or "winner" instead. This approach encourages growth and learning rather than sticking to negative labels that don't help you progress.

Blaming Yourself for Everything

Sometimes, it's easy to take the blame for everything bad that happens, even when it's not all your fault. Try to see the bigger picture and recognize that many factors contribute to different outcomes. Sharing responsibility, when appropriate, can help you see that you're not alone in making mistakes or facing challenges.

The Upside of Tackling Negative Thoughts

By understanding and actively working to shift these negative thought patterns, you don't just feel better in the moment—you also build skills for handling difficult situations in the future. Adjusting how you think about yourself and the events in your life helps you build a stronger, more confident self-image. Over time, this makes you more resilient and better equipped to handle life's ups and downs. Each step toward healthier thinking is a step toward becoming a happier, more balanced person.

INTERACTIVE ELEMENT: DEALING WITH YOUR TRIGGERS

In this activity, you'll engage in a personal exploration designed to help you identify and manage the specific triggers that provoke strong emotional reactions. This exercise will guide you through creating a detailed map of your emotional triggers, helping you to develop effective strategies for coping. The goal is to foster a deeper understanding of yourself and improve your ability to handle situations that have historically triggered stress or discomfort.

Objective: The aim of this exercise is to help you pinpoint the various external and internal triggers that affect your emotions. By recognizing these triggers, you can prepare to respond to them in healthier ways, ultimately enhancing your emotional resilience.

Materials Needed: You will need a notebook or digital device to record your observations (or you can use the space below). You will also want a quiet place and an open mind ready for introspection.

Instructions

Preparation

Find a comfortable and quiet space where you can reflect without interruptions. Ensure you have your notebook or digital device ready to document your insights.

Identification of Triggers

Situational Triggers: Think back to recent times when you felt upset, anxious, or unusually stressed. What was happening around you? Where were you, and who were you with? Document specific scenarios where your emotions felt more intense than usual.

____

____

____

____

____

Emotional Triggers: Reflect on the emotions that seem to consistently precede your feelings of distress. For example, does feeling overwhelmed often lead to anxiety? Do situations where you feel undervalued trigger sadness? Write down these emotional precursors.

____

____

____

____

____

Interpersonal Triggers: Consider if there are specific people or types of interactions that trigger negative emotions for you. Maybe certain conversations or social settings leave you feeling drained or irritable. Describe these interactions and note the people involved.

____

____

____

____

____

Recording Details: Create a structured list or chart in your notebook. Use categories like "Type of Trigger." "Specific Incident," "My Emotional Response," and "Potential Coping Strategy." This organization will help you clearly see patterns and correlations.

Fill in the chart with detailed descriptions of each incident, your emotional response, and think about potential healthy ways to cope with these triggers in the future.

Analyzing Patterns: Review your entries and look for patterns. Are there common themes or recurring scenarios? Do certain emotions frequently lead to discomfort or reactive behaviors?

Write a summary of your findings, reflecting on how these triggers impact your emotional well-being. Consider how you might change your reactions or your environment to better manage these triggers.

____

____

____

____

____

Developing Coping Strategies: For each type of trigger identified, brainstorm practical strategies that could mitigate your emotional response. For situational triggers, consider if there are ways to avoid the trigger, or prepare yourself better for unavoidable situations. For emotional triggers, list calming or grounding techniques you could employ, such as deep breathing, mindfulness, or physical activity.

____

____

____

For interpersonal triggers, think about setting boundaries or improving communication skills to manage these interactions more effectively.

Commitment to Action: Choose one or two strategies to focus on in the coming weeks. Set specific, achievable goals for how you will implement these strategies when faced with your identified triggers.

Plan a regular review of your progress. Adjust your strategies as needed based on what is working and what isn't.

Follow-Up: Return to this activity every few months to update your findings and refine your coping strategies. As you grow and change, your triggers and the best ways to handle them might also evolve. This ongoing process is a key part of managing your emotional health.

This activity encourages proactive engagement with your emotional landscape, empowering you to handle previously challenging situations with greater ease and confidence. By becoming more aware of what sets off your emotional responses and actively working to manage these triggers, you'll build a stronger foundation for emotional resilience and personal growth.

FINAL THOUGHTS

In this chapter, we explored the powerful impact of how your reactions to various situations shape your emotional well-being. We learned about Kaylie, a teenager who felt deep embarrassment and hurt after being the victim of a cruel prank at school. Initially, she experienced a natural mix of emotions—embarrassment, hurt, and anger, which are common in such painful situations. Over time, with guidance from her therapist, Kaylie discovered that, while we can't always control what happens to us, we have the power to control how we respond. It's our reactions to events, rather than the events themselves, that can either hurt or heal us.

We covered the importance of accepting all emotions, highlighting that every emotion, including those often considered negative like sadness or anger, has a purpose. These emotions act as signals about our environment and our needs. This understanding helps shift the perspective that there are no "bad" emotions; rather, it's how we respond to these emotions that matters.

The chapter also emphasized the skill of emotional regulation, which is not about suppressing feelings but rather understanding them and choosing responses that align with our values and long-term goals. This ability is crucial for personal development, helping us manage impulses and maintain self-esteem. For example, choosing to respond constructively to anger can build confidence in our ability to handle challenges effectively, boosting our self-perception.

Effective emotional management was discussed, including strategies such as recognizing and acknowledging emotions without judgment, identifying emotional triggers, and developing healthy coping mechanisms like talking to someone or engaging in physical activities. The practice of mindfulness was also highlighted as a tool to stay grounded in the present moment, helping to manage the intensity of emotions.

Additionally, we addressed the need for seeking help when emotions become overwhelming, reinforcing that it's okay to reach out for professional guidance to navigate complex emotional landscapes.

As we go from learning how to manage and understand our emotions, the next section will delve deeper into self-compassion and mindfulness. These practices are not merely about coping with difficult times; they are about transforming how we treat ourselves daily. By fostering a kinder, more compassionate relationship with ourselves, we enhance our capacity to appreciate life's positive moments and better navigate its challenges. This ongoing practice of self-care and emotional awareness leads to a more fulfilling and balanced life.

S
E
E
L-Love
F
I

CHAPTER 3

L—Love—Loving Yourself Unconditionally—Practicing Self-Compassion and Mindfulness

> *Talk to yourself as you would someone you love.*
>
> — BRENE BROWN

SELF-COMPASSION

In the last section, we looked at how our thoughts, especially the negative ones, play a huge role in shaping our feelings and reactions. Let's take that a bit further. Think about the last time you made a mistake, didn't do well on an exam, or didn't perform as expected in a competition. What went through your mind? Did you find yourself thinking harsh thoughts like "I'm so stupid," "I can't do anything right," or "I'm a failure"?

Now, try to imagine if you were talking to a friend or a family member who was in your shoes. Would you ever tell them they were stupid or a failure for slipping up or not coming out on top? Chances are, you wouldn't dream of it. You'd probably offer words of encouragement, remind them of their strengths, and help them see that it's not the end of the world. You'd be compassionate. So, why is it so hard to offer the same kindness to ourselves?

This is where the concept of self-compassion comes into play, and it's especially important for teens. Being a teenager isn't easy. You're at a stage where you're figuring out who you are, where you fit in, and dealing with all sorts of pressures—academic, social, and sometimes even at home. It's a time when self-compassion can really be a game-changer.

Self-compassion means treating yourself with the same kindness, concern, and support you'd naturally extend to a good friend. It's about being gentle with yourself when you're going through tough times or when you feel like you've failed. It involves recognizing that making mistakes and facing challenges is a part of life and a universal part of being human. Everyone goes through this—yes, even those who seem like they have everything figured out.

Let's talk about Rachel, a girl who always felt like she was not good enough. Despite studying hard, she once scored much lower than expected on a major exam. Her immediate thought was, "I'm such an idiot." But then, she remembered what she learned about self-compassion in a workshop at school. She paused, took a breath, and asked herself, "Would I say this to my best friend?" The answer was a resounding no. Instead, she told herself, "It's okay to be upset about this. It doesn't define me, and I can learn from it." This shift in thinking helped Rachel deal with her disappointment more constructively. Instead of spiraling into self-doubt, she reviewed what went wrong, figured out new strategies for studying, and reached out to her teacher for advice on what to focus on for the next test.

The shift toward self-compassion isn't just about feeling better in the moment; it's about building resilience. When you're compassionate with yourself, you're less likely to dwell on your past mistakes. This doesn't mean ignoring them but rather understanding them in a context that allows for growth and learning. It's about acknowledging that mistakes are not permanent reflections of your character but opportunities to improve and move forward.

Moreover, practicing self-compassion has been shown to reduce stress, anxiety, and even depression. It helps foster a healthier state of mind and equips you to handle future challenges with more grace and less judgment toward yourself. When you start treating yourself with the same care and respect you offer others, you not only improve your well-being but also create an inner strength that supports all areas of your life—from school to personal relationships.

So, the next time you find yourself being your own worst critic, take a pause. Imagine you're talking to a friend. Offer yourself the understanding and support you'd give them. This practice might feel a little awkward or difficult at first, but like any skill, it gets easier with practice. By incorporating self-compassion into your daily life, you'll be able to face challenges with a healthier, more supportive mindset, which is crucial during these formative years of your life.

WHY SELF-COMPASSION IS IMPORTANT, ESPECIALLY FOR TEENS

Self-compassion is a powerful and transformative practice, especially for teens navigating the complexities of adolescence. As mentioned above, it involves treating oneself with the same kindness, understanding, and patience that one would offer a close friend or family member in distress. This approach encourages individuals to acknowledge their own suffering, failures, and inadequacies without harsh judgment or self-criticism.

For teens, who are often dealing with academic pressures, social challenges, and intense emotional fluctuations, self-compassion can serve as a crucial lifeline. During these formative years, self-esteem and self-image are still developing, and negative experiences or feelings of inadequacy can be particularly damaging. Self-compassion provides a way to counteract this by promoting a healthier, more balanced view of oneself.

Understanding Self-Compassion

Self-compassion consists of three main components:

- **Self-Kindness vs. Self-Judgment:** This involves being warm and understanding toward oneself when experiencing pain or failure rather than being critical or harsh. It encourages recognizing that perfection is unattainable and that all humans are fallible and make mistakes. For a teen, this might mean accepting that not getting a perfect score or losing a game is not a reflection of their worth.

- **Common Humanity vs. Isolation**: This component recognizes that suffering and personal inadequacy are part of the shared human experience—something we all go through rather than something that happens to "me" alone. It helps teens see that they are not alone in their struggles; others are facing similar challenges.
- **Mindfulness vs. Overidentification**: Mindfulness in the context of self-compassion involves a balanced approach to negative emotions so that feelings are neither suppressed nor exaggerated. This balanced awareness is crucial in acknowledging and processing one's emotions healthily, without letting them define one's self-worth.

Why Self-Compassion Is Important for Teens

The teenage years are a period of significant psychological and emotional development. Research has shown that self-compassion can significantly improve mental health and well-being during this challenging phase. Here are some reasons why self-compassion is particularly beneficial for adolescents:

- **Reduces Anxiety and Depression**: Studies have found that self-compassion leads to lower levels of anxiety and depression. By cultivating a nonjudgmental understanding of one's own emotions and failures, teens can navigate stressful situations more calmly and with greater emotional resilience.
- **Enhances Self-Worth**: Self-compassion fosters a positive self-image by encouraging teens to acknowledge their strengths and weaknesses without self-reproach. This acceptance builds a more stable foundation of self-esteem that is less dependent on external successes or the approval of others.

- **Improves Emotional Resilience**: By recognizing and accepting their emotional experiences, teens learn to manage their feelings more effectively. This ability to cope with emotional distress plays a crucial role in maintaining mental health and adapting to life's challenges.
- **Promotes Healthy Relationships**: Self-compassion can lead to more empathetic and supportive relationships with others. Teens who are kind to themselves are more likely to extend that kindness to others, improving communication and understanding in relationships.
- **Encourages Personal Growth**: With a compassionate mindset, teens are more likely to view challenges and setbacks as opportunities for growth. This perspective encourages a proactive approach to learning and self-improvement rather than avoiding difficulties due to fear of failure.

Given these benefits, it's clear why integrating self-compassion into the lives of teens is essential. It not only equips them to handle the present challenges of adolescence but also lays the groundwork for a fulfilling and mentally healthy adulthood. By practicing self-compassion, teens can navigate their developmental years with more ease, understanding, and kindness toward themselves and others.

Embracing Self-Compassion

Self-compassion is a nurturing approach toward one's own experiences, especially when facing personal failings or difficult circumstances. It involves treating oneself with the same kindness, understanding, and support one would offer a friend in distress. For teenagers, developing self-compassion is particularly crucial due to the unique challenges this developmental stage presents, including identity formation, peer pressure, and academic stress. Embracing self-compassion can equip teens with tools to navigate these challenges more effectively, fostering a resilient and positive self-image.

Benefits of Practicing Self-Compassion

- **Promotes Acceptance**: Self-compassion encourages acceptance of one's flaws and shortcomings. For teens, this means learning to accept themselves as they are, without harsh judgments or undue criticism. This acceptance is fundamental to building a stable sense of self-worth that isn't easily shaken by external validations or failures.
- **Enhances Emotional Regulation**: By recognizing and responding to one's emotional needs with kindness, teens can better manage their emotional responses to stressful situations. Self-compassion helps in acknowledging painful emotions without becoming overwhelmed by them, which is a key component in effective emotional regulation. This skill allows adolescents to handle interpersonal conflicts and academic pressures with greater ease.
- **Encourages Self-Care**: Self-compassion inherently promotes self-care by valuing one's well-being. For teens, this might translate into taking time for activities that nurture their physical, emotional, and mental health, recognizing when they need a break, or seeking help when overwhelmed. Self-care driven by self-compassion leads to healthier lifestyle choices, such as adequate sleep, proper nutrition, and regular physical activity.
- **Reduces Stress**: Teens often face high levels of stress due to various pressures. Self-compassion can significantly mitigate this stress by changing the way they perceive and

interact with challenging situations. It provides an emotional buffer to handle stress more constructively, avoiding the pitfalls of self-criticism that often exacerbate stressful feelings.

- **Improves Mental Health**: Numerous studies have shown that self-compassion is strongly associated with reduced symptoms of anxiety and depression. It offers psychological stability by fostering a nonjudgmental and caring attitude toward oneself, which can be especially beneficial for teens navigating the emotional turbulence of adolescence.
- **Improves Physical Health**: There is a well-documented link between mental and physical health. Self-compassion not only enhances mental health but also contributes to better physical health. It can lead to lower levels of cortisol (the stress hormone) and reduced inflammatory responses, which are beneficial for overall health. Teens practicing self-compassion may experience fewer physical symptoms associated with stress and anxiety, such as headaches, fatigue, and sleep disturbances.
- **Increases Happiness:** Self-compassion opens the door to greater happiness and contentment. By reducing self-criticism and increasing self-acceptance, teens can enjoy an enhanced sense of overall well-being. This happiness is not contingent on achievements or failures but stems from an inner peace and acceptance of life's ups and downs.
- **Fosters Healthy Relationships**: Self-compassion fosters empathy, which can enhance interpersonal relationships. When teens treat themselves with compassion, they are more likely to extend the same kindness and understanding to others. This can lead to more supportive and satisfying relationships with peers, family members, and others in their social circle.

SELF-COMPASSION, MINDFULNESS, SELF-LOVE, AND SELF ESTEEM

Self-compassion is not just a nice-to-have quality; it's essential for healthy emotional development during adolescence—a critical period for laying the groundwork for adult mental health. Developing self-compassion helps teens build a reservoir of resilience that can protect against the psychological stresses that often emerge during these formative years. It encourages a mindful recognition of one's emotional state, promotes a balanced approach to one's imperfections, and fosters an empathetic attitude toward others.

Practicing self-compassion involves conscious steps such as pausing to assess one's emotional state, speaking to oneself with kindness in moments of distress, and recognizing that difficulties are a universal part of the human experience. It encourages teens to move away from unhealthy patterns of self-denial and self-criticism, instead guiding them toward more adaptive, supportive ways of handling life's challenges.

By having self-compassion, you not only enhance your current well-being but also set the stage for continued emotional growth and fulfillment into adulthood. In a world that often emphasizes competition and perfection, self-compassion stands out as a vital practice that promises greater emotional resilience, healthier relationships, and a more compassionate society.

Self-compassion, mindfulness, self-love, and self-esteem form a closely interlinked network that profoundly affects our mental and emotional health. Understanding these concepts in tandem offers a richer perspective on how we can cultivate a more fulfilling and mentally healthy life.

Self-Compassion and Mindfulness: A Symbiotic Relationship

Self-compassion and mindfulness are deeply interconnected, each enhancing and supporting the practice of the other. Mindfulness, which involves paying full attention to the present moment without judgment, allows us to become acutely aware of our thoughts and feelings. This heightened awareness is crucial for self-compassion, as it enables us to recognize our suffering without immediately reacting to it. When we are mindful of our emotional state, we can approach our feelings with the kindness and understanding that embody self-compassion.

Mindfulness provides the emotional space needed to observe our thoughts and feelings from a distance. This perspective helps us to detach from negative self-judgments and meet our experiences with compassion instead of criticism. For instance, if a teen is feeling overwhelmed by academic pressure, mindfulness allows them to acknowledge their stress without self-blame, and self-compassion offers comfort and understanding, reinforcing that it's okay to feel overwhelmed and that this doesn't reflect their worth or capabilities.

Mindfulness and Self-Esteem: Enhancing Self-Perception

The practice of mindfulness has a significant positive impact on self-esteem. By fostering an objective and nonjudgmental awareness of one's thoughts and emotions, mindfulness helps individuals disconnect their self-worth from their external achievements or failures. This detachment helps to stabilize self-esteem, as the individual's sense of self-worth becomes less vulnerable to fluctuations based on external circumstances.

Regular mindfulness practice encourages a consistent, accepting approach to one's experiences. It teaches that our value is not contingent on being perfect or always succeeding. This understanding is liberating and builds a more resilient and stable self-esteem. For example, a teenager might use mindfulness to notice thoughts that undermine their confidence and respond to these thoughts with understanding rather than criticism. This shift not only diminishes the power of negative thoughts but also reinforces a positive self-perception that is not easily shaken by life's ups and downs.

How Mindfulness Boosts Self-Confidence

Practicing mindfulness also directly influences self-confidence. It cultivates a greater awareness of one's inner resources, talents, and abilities. By being present and engaged, individuals can better appreciate their positive attributes and accomplishments, countering tendencies to focus solely on faults or failures. Mindfulness trains the mind to appreciate each moment and recognize the competencies we bring to our daily activities, which, in turn, enhances self-confidence. Teens, for instance, can apply mindfulness to become more aware of their unique skills and successes in various contexts, such as in schoolwork, hobbies, or relationships, reinforcing their confidence in their abilities.

Mindfulness and Self-Love: Nurturing a Positive Relationship with Oneself

Mindfulness also plays a crucial role in fostering self-love, which involves embracing oneself, flaws and all, with an open and accepting attitude. This acceptance is rooted in mindfulness, which promotes an awareness that is free of harsh judgments. As individuals practice mindfulness, they learn to treat themselves with the same kindness and care they would offer a loved one, which is the essence of self-love.

Self-love is about more than feeling good about oneself; it's about actively caring for and nurturing oneself. Mindfulness supports this by helping individuals recognize what they need to thrive, whether it's rest, connection, or self-expression, and encouraging actions that honor those needs.

The Interplay between Self-Love and Self-Compassion

While self-love focuses on fostering a positive relationship with oneself, self-compassion involves offering oneself understanding and kindness during times of suffering or perceived inadequacy. These concepts are deeply connected, as self-compassion can be seen as an action of self-love. Practicing self-compassion reinforces self-love by continually treating oneself with care and respect, especially in challenging times.

Together, self-love and self-compassion cultivate a nurturing internal environment that supports personal growth, emotional resilience, and a fulfilling life. They encourage a positive, accepting, and compassionate relationship with oneself, which is especially important during the teenage years when self-identity is still forming.

By understanding and practicing these interconnected concepts, teens can build a foundation of mental and emotional health that supports not only their personal development but also their relationships and academic and life successes. This holistic approach to mental health, centered around mindfulness, self-compassion, self-love, and healthy self-esteem, empowers teens to navigate their developmental years with confidence and resilience.

Self-compassion, mindfulness, self-love, and self-esteem form a closely interlinked network that profoundly affects our mental and emotional health. Understanding these concepts in tandem offers a richer perspective on how we can cultivate a more fulfilling and mentally healthy life.

BUILDING SELF-COMPASSION

Building self-compassion is like constructing a safe haven within yourself—a place where you can retreat, recharge, and remind yourself of your worth, especially when the going gets tough. Self-compassion isn't just about being nice to yourself; it's about being kind and understanding when confronted with personal failings or difficult situations, just as you would be to a friend in distress.

How to Practice Self-Compassion

Practicing self-compassion involves changing how you typically respond to yourself. Instead of harsh self-criticism, it requires nurturing a compassionate inner voice. This shift doesn't happen overnight, but through consistent practice, you can cultivate a more compassionate self-relationship. Here are several approaches:

- **Mindfulness**: Mindfulness is the bedrock of self-compassion. It allows you to observe your thoughts and feelings with openness and without judgment. Practicing mindfulness helps you recognize when you're slipping into self-criticism and instead steer toward compassionate thinking. Simple mindfulness exercises include paying attention to your breathing, noticing the sensations in your body, or observing your thoughts as they come and go without getting hooked by them.

- **Reframing Self-Critical Thoughts**: Start noticing when you're being self-critical and consciously choose to soften your internal dialogue. Replace critical or punitive thoughts with more understanding and supportive messages. For instance, change "I'm such a failure" to "Everyone makes mistakes, and I can learn from this."
- **Embrace Your Common Humanity**: Recognize that making mistakes and feeling inadequate at times is part of the shared human experience, not something that only happens to you. This perspective helps diminish the isolation often felt during times of failure and reinforces the understanding that you're not alone in your struggles.

Self-Compassion Exercises

To weave self-compassion into your daily life, here are a few exercises to try:

How Would You Treat a Friend?: Think of a time when a friend was struggling or made a mistake. What did you say to them? How did you comfort them? Now, imagine it was you in that situation. Try to extend the same compassion and understanding to yourself as you would to your friend. Feel free to use the space below.

____

____

____

____

____

Self-Compassion Break: Whenever you notice you're feeling stressed or down, take a moment to pause. Acknowledge that this is a difficult moment, feel the warmth of compassion flowing through your body, and speak kindly to yourself. Use phrases like, "May I give myself the compassion that I need."

Exploring Self-Compassion through Writing: Write a letter to yourself from the perspective of a compassionate friend. Let this friend highlight your strengths, forgive your mistakes, and offer encouraging words of wisdom. This exercise can be particularly powerful for gaining a new, more compassionate perspective on your own experiences.

____

____

____

____

____

Loving-Kindness Meditation: Start by sitting quietly and picturing someone you love. Send them wishes like, "May you be happy, may you be healthy." Gradually extend these wishes to yourself, then to acquaintances, and eventually to all beings everywhere. This practice helps cultivate a spirit of kindness and acceptance. You can use the space below to write your thoughts if you would like to.

____

____

____

____

____

Cultivating a Self-Compassionate Inner Dialogue: Change your critical self-talk into a kinder, more compassionate voice. Practice speaking to yourself in your mind as you would speak to someone you love deeply and respect. Write it down if you want to.

____

____

____

____

____

INTEGRATING SELF-COMPASSION INTO DAILY LIFE

To make self-compassion a daily practice, consider these steps:

- **Start Your Day with an Intention**: Each morning, set an intention to be kind and compassionate to yourself throughout the day. This can set a positive tone and remind you to react with kindness when challenges arise.

- **Carry This Intention with You:** Keep reminders of your intention to practice self-compassion. It could be a note on your phone, a bracelet, or a background image that reminds you to be gentle with yourself.
- **Take Baby Steps**: Integrate small acts of self-compassion into your routine. It could be taking five minutes to enjoy a cup of tea amid a stressful day or allowing yourself a moment to breathe when you feel overwhelmed.
- **Be Consistent:** Like any skill, self-compassion gets stronger with practice. The more you work at it, the more natural it will become.
- **Seek Support**: Share your journey toward self-compassion with friends or a mentor. They can offer encouragement, share their experiences, and help you stay on track.
- **Celebrate Progress**: Recognize and celebrate moments when you successfully practiced self-compassion. This recognition can reinforce the behavior and motivate you to continue.
- **Forgive Yourself:** Remember that the path to self-compassion is ongoing. If you slip back into self-criticism, forgive yourself and recommit to your practice.

HOW PRACTICING SELF-COMPASSION CAN HELP YOU ACHIEVE SUCCESS

Research shows that individuals who practice self-compassion are more likely to enjoy success. This is because they handle setbacks more constructively, see challenges as opportunities to grow, and recover from disappointments more quickly. Rather than getting bogged down by failures, they maintain a positive, hopeful outlook. This resilience not only contributes to better emotional health but also fosters a mindset that supports striving toward personal and academic goals.

Incorporating self-compassion into your life isn't just about feeling better in the short term—it's about building a robust framework for enduring success and well-being. As you continue to practice, you'll likely find that you're not only becoming more compassionate toward yourself but also enhancing your overall quality of life.

Being more mindful is about tuning into the present moment with full attention, without distraction or judgment. For teens, developing mindfulness can be particularly beneficial, helping them navigate the complexities of growing up with greater ease and awareness. Mindfulness practices can improve focus, reduce stress, and enhance emotional regulation, leading to a more balanced and fulfilling life.

A Simple Mindfulness Practice

A simple way to begin practicing mindfulness is to focus on your breath. Here's a basic exercise:

1. Find a quiet place where you can sit comfortably without being disturbed.
2. Close your eyes and take a few deep breaths to settle into the moment.
3. Begin to breathe normally and pay attention to the sensation of your breath as it enters and leaves your body. Notice how your chest and abdomen move with each breath.
4. When your mind wanders, gently bring your focus back to your breath.
5. Continue this practice for a few minutes, gradually increasing the time as you become more comfortable with the exercise.

Mindful Activities for Teens

Deep Breathing: This involves taking slow, deep breaths to help reduce stress and calm the mind.

How to do it:

1. Sit or lie down in a comfortable position. Inhale deeply through your nose, allowing your chest and lower belly to rise as you fill your lungs. Exhale slowly through your mouth or nose, depending on what feels more comfortable.

Paced Breathing: Helps regulate your breath and is especially useful during times of stress.

How to do it:

1. Breathe in for four seconds, hold the breath for four seconds, and exhale for four seconds.
2. Repeat this pattern for a few minutes.
3. Rest for one minute and repeat.

Progressive Muscle Relaxation: This technique involves tensing and then relaxing different muscle groups in the body, which can be very effective in releasing physical and mental tension.

How to do it:

1. Start by tensing the muscles in your feet for one minute.
2. Gradually work your way up to your head, tensing and relaxing each muscle group.
3. Relax for three minutes and repeat.

Meditation: Meditation can help center your thoughts and make you more aware of your mind-body connection.

How to do it:

1. Sit in a comfortable position, close your eyes, and focus on your breath.
2. Breathe slowly.
3. Slowly breath out.
4. When thoughts intrude, gently return your focus to your breathing.
5. Rest for two minutes and repeat.

Grounding with 5-4-3-2-1: This technique helps ground you in the present moment and is effective in managing anxiety.

How to do it:

1. Name five things you can see, four things you can touch, three things you can hear, two things you can smell, and one thing you can taste.
2. Focus on each one as you identify it.
3. Practice being in the present.

Body Scan: This involves paying attention to different parts of your body in turn, noticing any sensations or discomforts.

How to do it:

1. Lie down comfortably and slowly guide your attention through each part of your body, starting at your toes and moving upwards.
2. At each point, relax for at least two minutes.

Journaling: Writing down your thoughts and feelings can be a great way to deal with emotions mindfully.

How to do it:

1. Set aside a few minutes each day to write freely about your thoughts, feelings, or anything that's on your mind.
2. Be sure to focus on your feelings, good and bad, as you are writing.

Movement/Exercise: Physical activity is a great way to incorporate mindfulness, as it focuses on body movements and breathing.

How to do it:

1. Choose any form of exercise you enjoy, such as yoga, walking, or dancing, and focus closely on the movements and sensations of your body.
2. Concentrate on letting your stress out as you do your exercises.

Coloring and Listening to Music: Engaging in creative activities like coloring or listening to music can also be mindful practices. They help focus the mind and can be very relaxing.

How to do it:

1. Color or listen to music as usual but take in the sights, sounds, and beauty around you as you do.
2. Let your stress melt away.

Mindful Eating: This practice involves paying full attention to the experience of eating and drinking.

How to do it:

1. Before you eat, observe the food, taking in its colors and smells. While eating, chew slowly and savor each bite.
2. After eating, take a moment to notice how your body feels.

INTEGRATING MINDFULNESS INTO YOUR LIFE

Incorporating mindfulness into daily life doesn't have to be daunting. Start small by choosing activities you enjoy and practicing them regularly. Set a reminder to engage in these practices daily and find a time of day that works best for you—maybe morning or evening. Pair mindfulness practice with existing habits like brushing your teeth or waiting for a bus. Remember, consistency is key.

STICKING TO A MINDFULNESS PRACTICE

To make mindfulness a lasting part of your life, keep the practice enjoyable and manageable. Maybe start with just five minutes a day and gradually increase the time. Pairing it with an existing habit is helpful. Create a schedule for yourself and even write it on a calendar. Find a mindfulness buddy who can help keep you accountable, and don't forget to reward yourself for sticking with your practice. You can jot down your thoughts. If you miss a day, be compassionate with yourself and get back on track without self-criticism. Jot down ways you intend to help you in your practice of mindfulness.

____

____

____

____

____

MANIFESTING THE LIFE YOU WANT

Manifestation involves using your thoughts, feelings, and beliefs to bring something into your life. It's about focusing your energy on what you desire, whether it's achieving a goal or improving your relationships. Meditating on these things can help bring them to pass.

Many methods can be used when practicing manifestation, such as:

1. **Visualization**: Visualization involves creating a mental image of your desired outcome, which helps align your focus and energy with your goals. This practice encourages you to imagine success in vivid detail, enhancing motivation and clarity.
2. **Affirmations:** Affirmations are positive statements that reinforce your intentions and beliefs. Repeating affirmations daily can help reprogram your subconscious mind, fostering a mindset aligned with your desired outcomes.
3. **Gratitude:** Practicing gratitude shifts your focus to what you already have, creating a positive mindset that attracts

more abundance. Keeping a gratitude journal or simply expressing thanks daily can enhance your manifestation efforts.

4. **Vision Boards**: A vision board is a collage of images and words representing your goals and aspirations. Creating and regularly viewing a vision board helps maintain focus on your desires, reinforcing your commitment to achieving them.
5. **Scripting**: Scripting involves writing a story about your ideal future as if it has already happened. This technique engages your imagination and helps clarify your goals, making them feel more achievable.
6. **Meditation**: Meditation helps quiet the mind and enhances focus, creating space for intention setting and clarity. Regular meditation can improve your alignment with your desires and reduce negative thinking.

Self-compassion is crucial for effective manifestation because it fosters a positive and supportive mindset, which allows you to focus on your desires without self-doubt or criticism, thereby aligning your energy with your goals and enhancing your ability to attract what you want. As you see things manifest through your efforts, your confidence will grow. You will know that if you can dream it, you can make it happen.

INTERACTIVE ELEMENT: SELF-ESTEEM JOURNAL

Building self-esteem is an ongoing process that can be greatly enhanced through regular reflection and introspection. The Self-Esteem Journal is designed to facilitate this by providing a structured way for you to engage with your thoughts and feelings, celebrate your successes, and gently navigate your challenges.

Objective

This journal is a personal space where you can bolster your self-esteem by focusing on your strengths, accomplishments, and the progress you're making in various aspects of your life. It aims to shift your perspective from self-criticism to self-appreciation and encourages a more positive self-dialogue.

How It Works

The Self-Esteem Journal is divided into sections, each crafted to help you reflect on different aspects of self-esteem and personal growth. You will record daily entries that guide you to recognize your qualities, acknowledge your achievements, and embrace your challenges with a constructive and compassionate mindset.

SECTIONS OF THE SELF-ESTEEM JOURNAL

Today's Achievements

Description: Start by noting down the achievements of the day, no matter how small. These could include completing a task, making progress on a project, or managing to stay positive in a tough situation.

____

____

____

____

____

Purpose: This section helps shift the focus to your capabilities and successes, reinforcing a positive self-image and reminding you of your effectiveness and skills.

Challenges I Faced

Description: Reflect on any challenges or difficulties you encountered during the day. Describe what happened and how you felt, focusing on your reaction and coping strategies.

____

____

____

____

____

Purpose: By writing about challenges, you engage in problem-solving and can often find patterns in your responses that might be improved. This encourages resilience and emotional growth.

Lessons Learned

Description: Consider what you learned from the day's experiences, particularly from the challenges. Identify insights about how you might handle similar situations differently in the future.

____

____

____

____

____

Purpose: This section is crucial for personal development and helps you turn everyday experiences into learning opportunities, fostering a growth mindset.

Gratitude

Description: List at least three things you are grateful for today. These can be as simple as a sunny day, a friend's support, or something you enjoyed.

____

____

____

____

____

Purpose: Gratitude is strongly linked to increased happiness and a positive mood. By recognizing and appreciating the good in your life, you enhance your overall well-being.

Self-Compliment

Description: Give yourself a compliment each day. It should be something you genuinely feel good about, like a personal trait, a physical feature, or an action you took.

Purpose: This practice boosts self-love and acceptance, key components of high self-esteem. It also helps counter any negative self-talk.

Affirmations

Description: Write down positive affirmations that resonate with you. These should be present tense, positive statements that reinforce your self-worth.

Purpose: Affirmations can reprogram your subconscious mind to believe certain things about yourself, helping to create a positive identity and improve your self-esteem.

How to Get the Most out of Your Self-Esteem Journal

- **Consistency Is Key:** Try to write in your journal daily. Regular reflection maximizes the benefits of this practice.
- **Be Honest:** The more honest you are in your entries, the more you'll gain from this journal. It's a personal tool meant to foster growth, not to impress anyone.
- **Review Periodically:** Every month, take some time to review what you've written. This can help you see patterns, recognize growth, and adjust your focus if necessary.
- **Keep It Private:** Your journal is a private space. Keeping it confidential can help you feel safe to express yourself fully and honestly.

By maintaining a Self-Esteem Journal, you create a powerful tool for self-reflection and personal growth. Over time, this journal can become a cherished resource for understanding yourself better, learning from your experiences, and building a robust and resilient sense of self-worth.

FINAL THOUGHTS

In this chapter on loving yourself unconditionally through the practices of self-compassion and mindfulness, we dive into the importance of treating yourself with the same kindness and understanding that you would offer to someone you care about deeply. Imagine a scenario where you've stumbled or didn't meet your own expectations, like failing an exam or not performing well in a competition. Often, your first reaction might be to criticize yourself harshly. But, would you treat a friend that way? Probably not. You'd likely offer support and highlight their strengths, showing them compassion rather than judgment. This illustrates the essence of self-compassion, which is especially crucial during your teenage years—a time filled with challenges and changes.

Self-compassion involves recognizing that making mistakes and facing hardships are common human experiences. Everyone goes through tough times, even those who seem like they have everything under control. It's about allowing yourself to be imperfect and accepting yourself without harsh self-criticism. For instance, Rachel, a character we meet in this chapter, initially calls herself an idiot for not doing well on a test. However, by applying self-compassion, she reassures herself that one bad grade doesn't define her intelligence or her worth. This shift in mindset allows her to approach the situation with a clearer head, learning from her mistakes and planning better for future challenges.

Practicing self-compassion not only helps you in the moment of distress but also builds long-term resilience. It shifts how you relate to yourself fundamentally—instead of defaulting to self-criticism, you learn to nurture a supportive and understanding internal dialogue. This nurturing approach reduces stress, decreases feelings of anxiety and depression, and generally leads to a happier and more fulfilled life. You begin to see challenges as opportunities to grow and learn, rather than as insurmountable obstacles.

The practice of mindfulness complements self-compassion beautifully. Mindfulness teaches you to stay present and fully engage with the here and now, without overidentifying with your thoughts and emotions. It helps you notice when you're being too hard on yourself and allows you to adjust your internal conversation to be more supportive and kinder. Simple mindfulness exercises, like focusing on your breath or doing a body scan, can help anchor you in the present moment, making it easier to maintain a compassionate outlook toward yourself.

Incorporating mindfulness and self-compassion into your daily routine can be transformative. It could start with setting an intention each morning to be kind to yourself throughout the day, or it could involve more structured practices like journaling or meditating. The key is consistency. The more you practice, the more natural it becomes to approach yourself with compassion and understanding.

Lastly, this chapter highlights how these practices can help you manifest the life you want. By focusing on positive thoughts and goals, and supporting these with a compassionate mindset, you're more likely to take actions that align with your desires. Manifesting isn't just about wishing for what you want; it involves setting clear intentions, using your thoughts to guide your actions, and believing in your capacity to achieve your goals.

By embracing self-compassion and mindfulness, you're not just getting better at dealing with stress or setbacks; you're actively shaping a more positive, confident, and resilient version of yourself. In the next chapter, you'll learn about relationships and how to identify toxic ones and embrace healthy ones. This foundation will not only support you through your teenage years but also set you up for continued growth and happiness in adulthood.

S
E
E
I
F
L-Self-Love

CHAPTER 4

Building Healthy Relationships and Letting Go of Toxic People

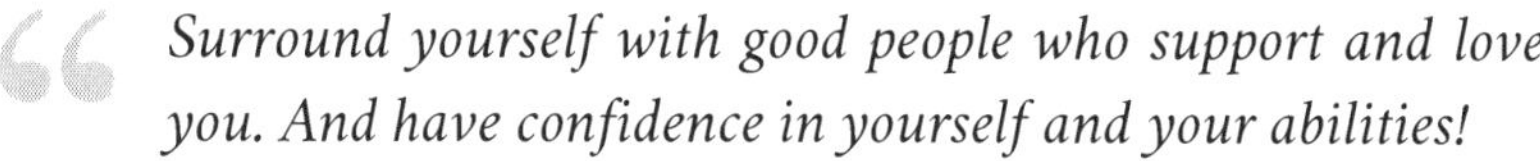

> *Surround yourself with good people who support and love you. And have confidence in yourself and your abilities!*
>
> — KIRSTIN MALDONADO

When you think about the people you hang out with, how do they make you feel? Do they lift you up, making you feel great about who you are, or do they push you down, as if you're not quite good enough? It's important to really consider this because the friends you choose to spend time with can greatly influence how you feel about yourself.

Friends should be your cheerleaders, not critics who make you feel like you have to prove yourself to earn their approval. When you're around the right people, you naturally feel more valued, worthy, and confident. True friends will celebrate your successes and help you through tough times, all without making you feel like you have to compete for their attention or friendship.

It's all about finding those who appreciate you for who you are, not just what you can do for them or how you make them look. Positive friendships will energize you and give you a sense of belonging. On the flip side, spending time with people who drag you down can really affect your self-esteem and how you view your own worth.

So, take a moment to think about it: Are your friendships lifting you up or weighing you down? Remember, you deserve to be around people who genuinely care for you and help you grow into the best version of yourself.

HOW CAN I IMPROVE MY SELF-ESTEEM?

Self-esteem is like a personal feeling of worthiness and confidence in one's own skin. It's about feeling good about yourself—feeling liked, accepted, and proud of what you do and believing in yourself. Unfortunately, not everyone naturally feels this way, and, sometimes, people struggle with low self-esteem, feeling overly critical about themselves and thinking they're not good enough.

UNDERSTANDING WHERE SELF-ESTEEM COMES FROM

Your self-esteem doesn't just appear out of nowhere—it's influenced by the events and people around you. Positive feedback and encouragement from others, like parents, teachers, and friends, can help you feel good about yourself. On the other hand, if you're often criticized or if you face bullying, it can really take a toll on how you see yourself. Another big influencer is the voice inside your head—what you tell yourself on a daily basis. If your inner voice is harsh, like constantly saying, "I'm such a loser" or "I'll never make friends," it's likely you'll start to believe it, and this harms your self-esteem.

Practical Ways to Boost Your Self-Esteem

- **Choose Your Company Wisely**: Surround yourself with people who treat you with kindness and respect, not those who bring you down. Having friends who support and uplift you can make a huge difference in how you view yourself.
- **Change Your Inner Dialogue**: Start listening to the things you say to yourself. Try writing down these thoughts for a few days and then reviewing them. Would you say these things to someone else you care about? If not, it's time to change those words into something more positive and encouraging.
- **Celebrate Your Efforts and Successes**: Give yourself credit for trying new things and achieving goals, no matter how small. Did you learn a part of a new song on the guitar? Did you improve your grades slightly in math? Celebrate those wins! Changing your focus from what you didn't do perfectly to recognizing your efforts builds self-esteem.
- **Accept Imperfection**: Nobody is perfect. Everyone makes mistakes, and that's okay—it's part of being human. Instead of beating yourself up for not being perfect, appreciate your effort. Each mistake is a step toward learning and growing.

- **Set Realistic Goals**: Setting clear, achievable goals gives you something to aim for and helps you measure progress along the way. Each achievement, no matter how small, will boost your confidence.
- **Focus on the Positives**: It's easy to dwell on problems or things that go wrong. Try shifting your focus to what goes well. Make a habit of identifying positive aspects of your day or your achievements. At the end of each day, think of at least three good things that happened.
- **Help Others**: Sometimes, boosting your self-esteem can be as simple as extending kindness to others. Helping someone else can make you feel good about yourself, increase your sense of worth, and make a positive difference in your community.

Remember, building self-esteem is a journey. It takes time, effort, and sometimes a bit of help from others, including friends, family, or even professionals like counselors. By understanding where your self-esteem issues stem from and taking active steps to improve how you feel about yourself, you can begin to see yourself in a more positive, realistic, and loving light.

THE POWER OF POSITIVITY IN TEEN LIFE

When navigating the complexities of adolescence, the people you choose to surround yourself with can profoundly influence your outlook on life and how you feel about yourself. Positive people aren't just happy themselves; they spread their optimism and joy to others, helping to bolster their friends' self-esteem and overall sense of well-being.

Positive friendships are more than just fun—they're vital to fostering a sense of self-confidence and belonging during your teenage years. Friends who are genuinely upbeat and supportive contribute to your personal growth and can help you navigate the ups and downs of life. They see the best in you, even when you might not see it yourself. They cheer you on, celebrate your victories, and stand by you during challenges.

Optimistic friends help you develop a positive mindset by modeling it themselves. They approach life with a can-do attitude and see setbacks as temporary and surmountable. This perspective can be incredibly contagious, encouraging you to adopt a similar outlook. When you're around positive people, you're more likely to embrace challenges and step out of your comfort zone, knowing you have a supportive circle that believes in your capabilities.

Positive Influence on Self-Esteem

One of the most significant benefits of having positive friends is the impact on your self-esteem. Positive individuals recognize that self-esteem doesn't diminish by sharing it. On the contrary, they understand that there's an endless supply and are always ready to build others up. This environment of mutual respect and affirmation is crucial during your teenage years when you're still forming your identity and learning to believe in yourself.

Having friends who are secure in themselves and supportive of you helps diminish the self-doubt that often comes with adolescence. They remind you of your worth and talents, especially when you forget. It's like having a personal cheer squad that roots for you no matter what.

Facing Setbacks with Confidence

Life, much like sales, as mentioned earlier, involves facing frequent rejections and setbacks. Each negative experience tests your resilience. Positive friends help you see these challenges as opportunities to grow rather than insurmountable obstacles. Their belief in your ability to bounce back and succeed provides an essential buffer against the harshness of teenage challenges.

Whether it's dealing with academic pressure, relationship issues, or personal insecurities, positive friends help you navigate these with a healthier outlook. They encourage persistence and offer perspectives that can turn a seemingly negative situation into a learning opportunity.

Choosing Your Circle Wisely

Choosing to spend time with positive people is a deliberate decision that can enrich your life immensely. Look for friends who are not only fun but also kind and nurturing. Notice how different friends make you feel about yourself and your decisions. Are they supportive? Do they celebrate your successes? Do they help you see the bright side of difficult situations? These are the people worth holding close to you.

It's equally important to distance yourself from those who drain your energy or continually bring negativity into your interactions. While it's normal for everyone to have a bad day, a pattern of pessimism can be harmful to your mental and emotional health.

Once you identify the positive influencers in your life, make an effort to strengthen these connections. Spend more time with them, engage in activities that you all enjoy, and support each other's goals and dreams. Positive relationships are a two-way street; as much as you benefit from their positivity, make sure to reciprocate with the same enthusiasm and support.

Remember, the goal isn't to have a perfect group of friends but to cultivate relationships that bring out the best in each other. By choosing positivity, you're not only enhancing your own life but also contributing to a happier, more supportive environment for everyone in your circle.

Navigating the world as a teenager can often feel like you're on a thrilling ride—sometimes exhilarating and other times overwhelming. Friendships during these years become not just a source of fun and company but also a significant influence on your personal identity and emotional growth.

The Impact of Friendships on Identity

For many teenagers, friendships are the lens through which they see themselves and the world. These relationships provide a platform for experimenting with different aspects of your personality and discovering more about who you are. Think about it—when you're with friends who appreciate the music you like, the style you wear, and even the quirky jokes you tell, you feel a sense of belonging. This validation is crucial, as it strengthens your sense of self and confirms that it's okay to be uniquely you.

However, the desire to fit in can sometimes be overpowering, leading to stress and pressure. It's common to worry about whether you're liked or accepted by your peers, and this can make you act differently or suppress what you truly think and feel. The fear of being left out or judged by friends can make anyone anxious, and, for teens, this can be particularly intense.

So, how do you balance these feelings? It starts with choosing the right friends—those who support you and encourage you to express your true self without fear of judgment. Positive friendships should make you feel good about being you, not make you feel like you have to change to be part of the group.

What Builds Positive Friendships?

Creating and maintaining healthy friendships involves more than just spending time together. It requires:

- **Respect**: True friends respect each other's opinions, feelings, and differences.
- **Support:** Good friends are there for each other, both on the good days and during tough times.
- **Honesty**: A strong friendship can withstand honesty. Being able to talk openly about what's bothering you is a sign of a healthy relationship.
- **Independence**: While it's great to have friends to share experiences with, it's also important to have your own interests and the ability to be alone sometimes. Dependency on friends for happiness is a common trap.

Dealing with Conflicts and Setbacks

Conflict is a normal part of any relationship, including friendships. Handling disagreements respectfully and effectively is crucial. Here are a few tips:

- **Communicate Clearly**: Instead of holding in resentment or anger, express your feelings calmly and clearly. Let your friend know why you are upset.

- **Listen:** Give your friend a chance to explain their side of the story.
- **Agree to Disagree**: Sometimes, you won't see eye to eye, and that's okay. Respecting each other's perspectives is key.

Embracing Your Individuality

Remember, while friends are a big part of your life, they don't define who you are. Embrace your interests, pursue your hobbies, and continue to make choices that are true to yourself. The right friends will respect and support your individuality.

Lastly, as you grow, it's natural to seek more independence. Balancing this desire with the safety and rules set by your parents can be tricky. Communication is key—discuss your need for independence with your parents, show them that you can make responsible choices, and gradually, they may give you more freedom.

Friendships in your teenage years are formative. They should help you feel confident, supported, and valued—not the opposite. By choosing friends wisely and learning to navigate the complexities of relationships, you can enhance your teenage years and develop into a well-rounded, happy adult.

WHAT GENUINE FRIENDSHIPS LOOK LIKE

Navigating friendships during your teenage years can be complex, but understanding what genuine friendships look like can guide you toward more fulfilling and supportive relationships. Real friendships—those that provide joy, support, and growth—have certain traits that set them apart from more superficial connections.

- **Supportive and Encouraging:** A true friend stands by your side not just during the good times but also when challenges arise. Support from a friend comes in many forms, whether it's listening to your worries, helping you with homework, or standing up for you when someone treats you unfairly. Genuine friends provide a steady source of support and encouragement, pushing you toward personal growth and cheering on your efforts, no matter how big or small.
- **Celebratory and Compassionate:** Real friends celebrate your successes without hesitation or jealousy. When you score the winning goal, ace a test, or get accepted into a college, they revel in your happiness as if it were their own. Conversely, during tougher times—such as a family crisis or personal setback—a true friend offers a shoulder to cry on. They provide comfort and empathy, helping you navigate through your defeats without making you feel like a burden.
- **Unconditional Love and Trust:** Unconditional love forms the foundation of any genuine friendship. Friends who love you unconditionally appreciate you for who you are, not just for your achievements or what you can offer them. This kind of friend sticks with you, believing in your worth and abilities, even when you doubt yourself. Trust is also crucial; it ensures that secrets shared in confidence stay that way and that the vulnerability shown during tough times isn't taken advantage of.
- **Respectful and Honest:** True friends respect your opinions and feelings. They appreciate your differences and see them as qualities that make you unique, not faults that need to be corrected. Honesty is also vital in genuine friendships—it builds trust and deepens the connection. An honest friend will tell you when you've made a mistake,

but in a way that is constructive and caring, rather than critical and hurtful.

- **Available and Present:** In an age where everyone seems perpetually busy, genuine friends make time for each other. It doesn't always have to be about grand gestures or long hours spent together; sometimes, it's just a quick check-in to see how you're doing or a spontaneous ice cream run. Being present also means that when you're together, they're not constantly distracted or looking over your shoulder for someone better to come along. They are fully engaged and appreciative of the time spent with you.
- **Happiness and Positivity:** Genuine friends should make you feel happy and positive about life. They bring laughter, joy, and positivity into your days. They help you see the brighter side of life and encourage you to do the same. A real friend enriches your life and uplifts your spirits; they don't drag you down with negativity or pessimism.
- **Doesn't Sabotage Your Happiness:** A true friend will never intentionally sabotage your happiness. If they hear rumors or negative comments about you, they won't spread them; instead, they will defend you and ensure you are treated fairly. They are loyal and protect your interests, especially when you're not around to defend yourself.

In essence, genuine friendships are those that bring out the best in you. They are rooted in mutual respect, support, and understanding. As you grow and navigate the complexities of teenage life, strive to cultivate friendships that embody these characteristics. Not only will they enhance your life, but they will also provide a stable foundation of support as you explore the world and your place within it.

TOXIC RELATIONSHIPS

Dealing with teenage friendships can be quite a challenge. While friendships can be sources of joy and support, they can also veer into less healthy territory. Recognizing the signs of toxic relationships and understanding how to handle them can make a significant difference in your social life and overall well-being.

Understanding Frenemies and Toxic Friendships

The term "frenemies" refers to those who might seem like friends on the surface but often exhibit behaviors that can be hurtful or mean. They might be part of your social circle and appear friendly at times, but their actions can sometimes leave you feeling betrayed or undermined. Recognizing these relationships is crucial because they can often lead to feelings of confusion, hurt, and low self-esteem.

Toxic friendships are similarly harmful. These relationships are characterized by consistent negativity and a lack of support and can make you feel worse about yourself rather than better. Such friends might belittle your achievements, spread or believe rumors about you, or fail to respect your boundaries. These friendships drain energy and can significantly impact your mental health.

Managing and Ending Toxic Friendships

If you find yourself in a friendship that feels more draining than supportive, it's important to consider taking steps to address or possibly end this toxic relationship.

- **Communicate Your Feelings**: Sometimes, friends are unaware of the impact of their actions. Have an honest conversation about how you feel and what you need from the relationship. Use "I" statements to express your feelings without sounding accusatory.
- **Set Boundaries:** Clearly define what behaviors you find unacceptable and what you expect from your friends. Setting boundaries is crucial for any healthy relationship and helps ensure mutual respect.
- **Seek Support**: Talk to trusted adults, counselors, or other friends about your experiences. They can offer advice, support, and a different perspective on the situation.
- **Decide If It's Time to Move On**: If the relationship continues to hurt your well-being despite your efforts to fix it, it might be time to consider ending it. You deserve friendships that make you feel good about yourself, not ones that leave you feeling insecure or unhappy.
- **Find New Friends**: Look for peers who share your interests and values. Join clubs, sports teams, or other activities where you can meet new people who might become friends.

Building New Friendships

Exploring new friendships can be intimidating but also incredibly rewarding. Start by joining groups that align with your interests, whether it's a school club, sports team, or community group. These venues provide opportunities to meet others with similar passions, making it easier to form connections that could turn into lasting friendships.

Friendships—like all relationships—require effort, trust, and communication. While it can be challenging to navigate the complexities of social interactions during your teen years, understanding what makes a friendship healthy can guide you toward more fulfilling connections. Seek out friends who enrich your life and offer the support, respect, and positivity everyone deserves in a friendship.

Dealing with Social Confidence Issues and Social Anxiety

Many teenagers struggle with social confidence and anxiety, which can significantly impact their ability to form and maintain friendships. Understanding and addressing these issues is crucial to helping you feel more secure in your social interactions.

- **Understanding Social Anxiety:** Social anxiety is more than just shyness; it's a persistent fear of being judged or embarrassed in social situations. This can make everyday interactions feel daunting. Managing social anxiety involves recognizing your feelings, understanding the triggers, and developing strategies to cope with them effectively. Strategies might include practicing relaxation techniques such as deep breathing or meditation, preparing for social interactions by role-playing conversations, or gradually facing social situations you fear in a controlled and manageable way.
- **Boosting Social Confidence:** Improving your social confidence can start with small, manageable steps. Begin by setting simple goals, such as initiating conversations with peers or joining a group activity. Acknowledge and celebrate small victories along the way to build your confidence. Additionally, educating yourself about social

dynamics and communication skills can empower you to interact more confidently.

How to Maintain Friendships and Be a Good Friend

Maintaining friendships requires effort and intention. Being a good friend involves showing up for others, listening intently, offering support, and expressing genuine interest in their lives. It's important to communicate openly and regularly, share experiences, and make time for each other. Also, be aware of your friends' needs and boundaries, and ensure you respect them, as this is fundamental to sustaining healthy and supportive friendships.

Understanding Conflicts

Conflicts are a normal part of any relationship, including friendships. Understanding how to manage conflicts can prevent them from escalating and damaging the relationship.

Recognize that conflict is not necessarily negative and can be a catalyst for growth and understanding within a relationship. Conflicts can arise from misunderstandings, differences in perspective, or competing needs. It's essential to address these issues openly rather than avoid them to maintain healthy relationships.

Conflicts among teens often revolve around misunderstandings, jealousy, breaches of trust, or differences in values. Identifying the type of conflict you are dealing with can help in finding the most appropriate solution.

Key Steps in Conflict Resolution

- **Active Listening and Empathy**: Listen carefully to the other person's perspective without interrupting. Try to understand their feelings and viewpoints and show empathy, which can help de-escalate tensions.
- **Assertiveness and Effective Communication**: Express your own feelings and needs clearly and respectfully without being passive or aggressive. Use "I" statements to focus on your feelings rather than accusing the other person.
- **Tips for Effective Conflict Resolution**: Seek to find common ground or a compromise where both parties can agree. Be willing to apologize if you've made a mistake or hurt the other person, even if unintentionally. Sometimes, it may be helpful to involve a neutral third party to mediate the conflict, especially if it escalates.

INTERACTIVE ELEMENT: PUTTING WHAT YOU'VE LEARNED INTO PRACTICE

An "I statement" is a way to express your feelings clearly and directly without blaming others or escalating tensions. It's particularly useful in delicate situations where you need to convey what's bothering you while maintaining respect and understanding.

The Structure of an "I Statement"

Creating an effective "I statement" involves three key parts:

- **I Feel:** Start by explicitly stating your emotion. This focuses the conversation on your personal feelings and avoids casting blame.

Example: "I feel overwhelmed."

- **When**: Clearly describe the behavior or situation that triggered this feeling. This helps the other person understand the context of your emotions.

Example: "The problem is homework piling up right before the weekend."

Next Time, I Want: Stating a positive change you'd like to see. This provides a clear expectation of how you wish to be treated or what actions you prefer to be taken.

Example: "To avoid homework piling up just before the weekend, next time I want to discuss our plans earlier in the week to manage my workload better."

Practice Creating Your Own "I Statement"

Reflect on a recent incident where you felt a strong emotion due to someone else's actions. Using the structure provided, formulate your own "I statement" to articulate your feelings, the cause, and your desired change for future interactions.

Example:

I FEEL ignored

WHEN messages in our group chat go unanswered, especially when I'm seeking advice.

NEXT TIME, I WANT us to try to acknowledge each other's messages, even if it's just to say we'll get back to it later.

Your Turn:

I feel ____

When ____

Next time, I want ___________________________________

By using "I statements," you take ownership of your emotions and clearly communicate your needs, paving the way for healthier and more effective interactions.

FINAL THOUGHTS

Reflecting on this chapter about friendships during your teenage years, we've looked at what makes friendships really good and supportive and what signs show that a friendship might actually be harmful. Good friends are there for you—they cheer you on when you do well and help you feel better when things don't go your way. We've also learned about toxic friendships, where things like jealousy and manipulation can make you feel really bad about yourself.

We talked about how to express your feelings better using "I statements," which help you say what's on your mind without making someone defensive or starting an argument. Plus, we went over ways to deal with feeling nervous or shy around people, like taking small steps to feel more comfortable and confident in social settings.

Next, we're going to dive into a really important topic: dealing with the need to be perfect all the time. This part, called "Conquering Perfectionism: Embracing Flaws and Overcoming Low Self-Esteem," will help you see that it's okay to not always get everything right. We'll go over how feeling like you have to be perfect can make you stressed, and how learning to be okay with not being perfect can make you feel a lot better about yourself.

We'll get into some easy ways to start feeling better about who you are, like recognizing what you're good at and giving yourself a break when things don't go perfectly. These steps are not just about making friends or getting along with others—they're about feeling better about yourself and tackling everyday challenges with more confidence.

S
E
E
L
I
F-Flaws

CHAPTER 5

F—Flaws—Conquering Perfectionism—Embracing Flaws

Striving for excellence motivates you; striving for perfection is demoralizing.

— HARRIET B. BRAIKER

PERFECTIONISM IS TRENDING, AND IT'S NOT A GOOD THING

Lately, there's been a noticeable increase in perfectionism among young people, especially in places like the United States, Canada, and the United Kingdom, where there's a lot of pressure to stand out and be the best. This push to be perfect in everything, from grades to looks, can really affect your mental health.

Since the 1980s, society has really started to value individual competition—basically, everyone is trying to outdo each other. Think about it like everyone feeling they have to top their friends' Instagram posts or be the star athlete and top student. Studies tracking thousands of students over nearly thirty years have found that not only are teens feeling pressure to be perfect themselves, but they also feel like everyone expects them to be perfect, and they even expect perfection from others around them.

What Happens When You Try to Be Perfect All the Time?

Trying to meet these super-high standards all the time can lead to serious stress. One of the biggest problems with perfectionism is that it can lead to feelings of sadness, depression, and even suicide. Constantly feeling like you're not good enough because you're not reaching these impossible standards can really wear you down.

Eating disorders are another major issue linked to perfectionism. When you're really hard on yourself about meeting high standards, you might start focusing too much on controlling your diet and appearance. Research shows that worrying a lot about avoiding failure and being overly critical of yourself (what experts call "perfectionistic concerns") is more likely to lead to eating disorders than just trying to do your best (known as "perfectionistic strivings").

How Can You Deal with the Pressure of Being Perfect?

Knowing about the traps of perfectionism can help you manage the pressure better. Here are some tips:

- **Learn the Signs**: Get to know what unhealthy perfectionism looks like. Are you freaking out over every small mistake? Do you beat yourself up if everything isn't just right? These might be signs you're falling into the perfectionism trap.
- **Talk about It:** Whether it's with friends, family, or a counselor, talking helps. Sometimes just saying what's bothering you out loud can make a big difference.
- **Join Groups or Workshops:** Some schools or community centers have groups where you can meet other teens dealing with the same pressures. It can be really reassuring to hear that others are feeling the same way.
- **Focus on What You Enjoy:** Instead of worrying about being perfect in everything, find activities you really like and focus on enjoying them, not being the best at them.

Remember, It's Okay Not to Be Perfect

Really, it's okay! Everyone makes mistakes, and no one is perfect, no matter how it might look from the outside. Instead of getting hung up on what you think you're doing wrong, try to think about things you've done well. Focus on your strengths and give yourself a break. Getting involved in sports, arts, or volunteering can also help boost your confidence and show you that your value isn't based just on achievements.

Understanding and dealing with perfectionism isn't just about feeling better now—it's about setting yourself up for a healthier mindset in the future. So take a breath and remember that you don't have to be perfect to be amazing.

WHAT IS PERFECTIONISM?

Perfectionism isn't just about trying to do well; it's an intense drive to achieve absolute perfection in everything you do. This pressure can seep into every aspect of your life, from schoolwork to sports to how you present yourself on social media.

Signs and Symptoms of Perfectionism

Here are some of the most common signs and symptoms teens with perfectionism have:

- **Fear of Failure**: One of the clearest signs of perfectionism is an overwhelming fear of failing. This fear can be so strong that it stops you from trying new things or taking any risks, just in case you might not succeed.
- **Highly Self-Critical:** Perfectionists often have a harsh inner critic. You might find yourself constantly picking apart everything you do, focusing only on the flaws, and never feeling satisfied with your achievements.
- **All-or-Nothing Thinking:** This kind of thinking means seeing things in extremes. If something isn't done perfectly, it's a total failure. There's no middle ground or room for mistakes, which can make even small tasks feel daunting.
- **Persistent Striving for Perfection:** Even when perfectionists achieve their goals, they don't stop and celebrate. Instead, they immediately set another, higher

goal. It's a never-ending cycle of striving for something just out of reach.

- **Anxiety and Stress:** All this pressure can lead to high levels of stress and anxiety. Worrying constantly about meeting high standards and fearing judgment from others can make everyday life stressful and exhausting.

MANAGING PERFECTIONISM

Recognizing these signs in yourself is the first step toward managing perfectionism. Once you see these patterns, you can start working on strategies to cope. It's important to set realistic goals and celebrate small successes along the way. Learning to accept and learn from mistakes can also help reduce the anxiety that comes with perfectionism. Sometimes, talking to a counselor or therapist can be very helpful in working through perfectionist tendencies.

The goal isn't to stop striving to do well; it's to find a healthier balance and enjoy the journey, not just the destination. Recognizing that perfection is an impossible standard can free you to celebrate your efforts and achievements without the shadow of self-criticism. This shift in perspective can significantly reduce the stress and anxiety associated with perfectionism, leading to a more balanced and fulfilling life.

In today's world, teens face an immense amount of pressure to achieve perfection across various aspects of life, whether it's in academics, appearance, or social media presence. This drive toward perfectionism, deeply ingrained in our culture, often starts from a positive place—the desire to succeed. However, when striving for flawlessness becomes a relentless pursuit, it can have detrimental effects.

From the 1980s onwards, societies in countries like the United States, Canada, and the United Kingdom have increasingly valued competitive individualism. As a result, young people feel a compelling need to perfect themselves and their lifestyles, not just to stand out but often just to keep up. This pressure can turn destructive, morphing goals into unrealistic expectations.

Perfectionism, especially in teens, often manifests as an intense fear of making mistakes. If you find yourself hesitating to try new things for fear of failing or constantly critiquing your performance harshly, you might be slipping into perfectionistic patterns. This mindset can lead to significant stress and anxiety, as the fear of not being good enough becomes all-consuming.

The effects of this perfectionism are far-reaching. Studies indicate that it can lead to serious mental health issues, including depression, anxiety, and eating disorders. The fear of failure and the relentless self-criticism associated with perfectionism can prevent you from engaging in challenging opportunities and reduce your overall quality of life.

It's also evident in social settings. On platforms like Instagram and YouTube, where influencers often showcase idealized versions of life, the pressure to emulate these seemingly perfect lives can be overwhelming. You might find yourself making comparisons that detract from your self-esteem, pushing you further into the perfectionism trap.

Addressing this issue involves a shift in perspective. Recognizing that perfection is an unattainable goal is crucial. Instead of aiming for perfection, focus on progress and personal growth. Embrace mistakes as opportunities for learning rather than signs of failure. This mindset can alleviate the pressure that comes with perfectionism and lead to a more balanced and fulfilling life.

Encouragement from parents and educators can also play a pivotal role. Instead of emphasizing perfect outcomes, they should celebrate the effort and resilience shown in the face of challenges. This approach helps build a sense of worth that is based on real-life skills rather than unachievable standards.

Ultimately, overcoming the pitfalls of perfectionism is about understanding that it's okay not to be perfect. Learning to accept yourself, flaws and all, can foster genuine self-esteem and allow you to engage with life in a healthier, more positive way. So, take a step back from the relentless pursuit of perfection and give yourself the space to grow, make mistakes, and find joy in the imperfections that make you unique.

Perfectionism, often seen as a relentless drive to achieve flawless outcomes, can significantly impact various aspects of an individual's life, particularly in relation to self-esteem. While striving for excellence can be positive, when it shifts into perfectionism, it can create more problems than it solves. This intense pursuit of the ideal often leads to a range of negative outcomes that can affect mental health, personal growth, and overall well-being.

Perfectionism is a big issue, especially for teenage girls. It often shows up in different ways—like in school, sports, or hanging out with friends—where the fear of making mistakes can stop you from trying new things. Many girls worry a lot about what others think if they mess up. This can really stress you out because you might feel like you have to avoid any mistakes to not be judged. It's important to know that it's okay to make mistakes—they're part of learning and getting better at anything you do. We need to create spaces where it's cool to take on challenges and see that it's normal to not always get things right the first time.

The Link between Perfectionism and Self-Esteem

Self-esteem is how we value and perceive ourselves. It's shaped by our experiences, achievements, and the feedback we receive from others. Perfectionism can severely undercut self-esteem by setting an impossibly high bar for success. When perfectionists fail to meet these unrealistic standards, which is inevitably often the case, it can lead to feelings of inadequacy and self-doubt.

Perfectionism can turn every task—whether it's a school project, a personal goal, or even daily routines—into a potential failure point. This is because the standards set are so high that they are almost always out of reach. The constant fear of not meeting these standards can paralyze perfectionists, making them hypercritical of their every action and overly dependent on external validation. This reliance on achieving to feel worthy can erode self-esteem, giving way to a whole host of negative implications.

The Negative Impacts of Perfectionism

Perfectionism can have negative side-effects, such as:

- **Low Self-Esteem:** Constantly falling short of one's own unattainable standards can lead to pervasive feelings of incompetence. This, in turn, deeply impacts an individual's self-esteem, as they start to see themselves as perpetual failures, regardless of their actual successes and strengths.
- **Risk-Averse:** The fear of failure often makes perfectionists risk-averse. Avoiding new challenges helps guard against the possibility of failing, but it also hinders growth and learning. By not venturing out of their comfort zones, perfectionists can miss out on important opportunities for personal and professional development.

- **Overly Critical:** Perfectionists tend to be excessively critical of themselves and, at times, of others. This criticism can be debilitating, stifling creativity and spontaneity. Being overly critical can strain relationships and lead to a stressful environment where it's difficult to feel joy and satisfaction.
- **Procrastination:** Ironically, the fear of not being perfect can lead to procrastination. Perfectionists often delay starting projects because they fear they won't be able to complete them perfectly. This procrastination can lead to a vicious cycle of stress, last-minute rushes, and dissatisfaction with the end product, reinforcing feelings of inadequacy.
- **Failure to Learn:** Failure is an important teacher. However, for those caught in the trap of perfectionism, failure is seen not as an opportunity to learn but as a sign of incompetence. This view prevents them from taking valuable lessons from experiences that don't go as planned, stunting their personal growth and adaptability.
- **Poor Health:** The chronic stress associated with perfectionism can lead to serious health problems, including anxiety, depression, eating disorders, and even physical issues such as chronic headaches or heart problems. The constant strain of striving for perfection puts immense pressure on both the mind and body, leading to long-term health consequences.

Addressing the Challenges of Perfectionism

Overcoming the challenges posed by perfectionism involves recognizing the harmful patterns and actively working to change them. Setting more realistic goals, celebrating small successes, learning to accept and embrace imperfections, and seeking professional help if needed can all be part of building a healthier approach to achievements and self-evaluation.

Learning to value effort over perfection, focusing on personal progress, and understanding that mistakes are a natural part of learning and growth can help mitigate the negative effects of perfectionism. By redefining success and what it means to be competent, individuals can improve their self-esteem and lead richer, more fulfilling lives that aren't overshadowed by the pursuit of perfection.

Dealing with perfectionism isn't about lowering your standards, but about being kinder to yourself and realizing that your worth isn't tied to being perfect. By understanding where this pressure comes from and finding healthy ways to handle it, you can start feeling better about yourself and enjoy life more.

Perfectionism is a common struggle among teens, and it often stems from feeling like your self-worth is tied to your achievements. It's like you're constantly under pressure to perform perfectly in every test, match, or social setting, which can be exhausting.

Sometimes this pressure comes from the idea that achieving great things is the only way to earn acceptance, love, and praise. You might see perfection as a ticket to fitting in or standing out in a positive way.

What Perfectionism Feels Like

Being a perfectionist might mean you're really tough on yourself. If you get a B instead of an A, it feels like a huge letdown, even if a B is a good grade. You might avoid trying new things if you think there's a chance you won't excel at them right away. This is because the fear of failure is really intense and seems like something to avoid at all costs.

Often, the drive to be perfect is fueled by pressure from parents or teachers, who might focus a lot on grades and achievements. They might not mean to stress you out, but their high expectations can make you feel like you need to be perfect to be valued.

Social media can also make you feel like you need to live a perfect life. Scrolling through pictures and posts where everyone seems happy, successful, and flawless can make you feel like you need to match that standard.

The Impact on Your Mental Health

Trying to live up to these high standards can lead to anxiety and stress. It can make you overly critical of yourself and others and push you to procrastinate on tasks out of fear of not doing them perfectly. Over time, this stress can even affect your physical health, leading to things like headaches, sleep problems, or eating disorders.

Moving beyond Perfectionism

It's important to recognize that being perfect at everything is not only unrealistic but also unnecessary. It's okay to strive to do well, but not at the cost of your happiness or health. Learning to accept and learn from mistakes can be a huge relief. Remember, everyone makes mistakes—even those who seem perfect on Instagram or YouTube.

Taking the pressure off doesn't mean you don't try to do well; it just means you don't let fear of imperfection stop you from enjoying life and trying new things. Focusing on effort rather than perfection can help you feel more satisfied with your achievements and reduce the anxiety associated with needing to be perfect.

Exploring these issues and understanding how to manage the pressure to be perfect can make a big difference in how you feel about yourself and how you handle challenges. It's about finding a balance that allows you to be happy and healthy while still achieving your goals.

HOW TO OVERCOME PERFECTIONISM

Overcoming perfectionism is a valuable skill that can improve your mental health and overall quality of life. Here's a detailed guide on how to recognize and address perfectionistic tendencies, enabling you to embrace a more balanced approach to life.

Step 1: Learning to Recognize Perfectionism

Understanding Perfectionism

Perfectionism often begins with a deep-seated belief that your worth is directly linked to your performance, accomplishments, and ability to achieve flawless results. This belief can be debilitating, leading to a relentless pursuit of perfection at the expense of your happiness and well-being.

Examples of Perfectionistic Feelings

Feeling inadequate despite successes, persistent dissatisfaction with oneself, and a lingering sense that nothing you do is quite good enough are common emotional markers of perfectionism.

These feelings can fuel a continuous cycle of self-doubt and frustration.

Examples of Perfectionistic Thinking

- **Black-and-White Thinking**: You see things in extremes. If a project isn't perfect, it's a complete failure.
- **Catastrophic Thinking**: You anticipate the worst possible outcomes, especially from minor mistakes.
- **Probability Overestimation**: You might overestimate the likelihood that something bad will happen, like thinking you'll fail an entire course because of one bad grade.
- **Should Statements**: You have a rigid code of conduct dominated by "shoulds," "musts," or "oughts," which can create unrealistic expectations for yourself and others.

Examples of Perfectionistic Behavior

Perfectionists often engage in excessive checking, procrastinating due to a fear of not doing something perfectly, or repeatedly trying to perfect something at the cost of their time and mental health. They might avoid tasks where they fear failure or constantly seek reassurance due to self-doubt.

Step 2: Tools to Overcome Perfectionism

Tool #1: Changing Perfectionistic Thinking

- **Realistic Thinking**: Challenge your perfectionistic thoughts. Replace thoughts like "It needs to be perfect" with "It's good to do my best."
- **Perspective Taking**: Ask yourself, "What would I tell a friend in this situation?" Often, you'll find that you are much harsher on yourself than on others.

- **Looking at the Big Picture:** Will this matter in a week, a month, or a year? Focusing on the big picture can help reduce the pressure you put on any one event or task.
- **Compromising**: Find a middle ground. If your standards are unreachably high, adjust them to more practical, achievable levels.

Tool #2: Changing Perfectionistic Behaviors

Start by setting more realistic goals and celebrating small victories along the way. Gradually expose yourself to situations where outcomes are uncertain or where you might not perform perfectly. This exposure can help reduce the anxiety associated with potential failure.

Tool #3: Overcoming Procrastination

Procrastination is often a byproduct of fearing failure. To overcome this, break tasks into smaller, manageable parts and set clear deadlines for each part. Focus on starting tasks rather than finishing them perfectly. This approach reduces the overwhelming feeling that can come with big projects.

Step 3: Reward Yourself

Recognizing and rewarding your efforts rather than outcomes can shift your focus from perfection to progress. Treat yourself after completing a task, even if the result isn't perfect. This could be something as simple as taking a break, enjoying a favorite snack, or spending time on a hobby. Rewards reinforce positive behavior and help build new, healthier habits.

Overcoming perfectionism isn't about lowering your standards but about learning to pursue excellence in a healthy way that doesn't compromise your mental health. It involves recognizing the signs of unhealthy perfectionism, actively changing destructive thoughts and behaviors, and learning to appreciate and reward effort over flawless outcomes. This journey can lead you to a happier, more fulfilling life, where success is measured not by perfection but by your ability to embrace and learn from all experiences.

Perfectionism and body image are closely intertwined, especially during the teenage years. As you grow and your body changes, the pressure to look a certain way can sometimes feel overwhelming. This pressure often stems from a variety of sources and can profoundly affect how you see and feel about yourself.

UNDERSTANDING BODY IMAGE

Body image refers to how you see your physical self—whether you see yourself as attractive or not—and how that perception makes you feel. This can be influenced by your own beliefs and also by reactions from others.

Perfectionism and Body Image

Perfectionist thinking can severely impact body image. If you're always striving to meet unrealistically high standards, you might start feeling negative about your body if it doesn't "measure up." These feelings can be amplified by the images and messages you see in the media, which often highlight idealized and unattainable body types.

Causes of Body Image Issues

Some of the most common causes of feeling poorly about your body image are:

Media and Social Media

One of the biggest influences on body image is the media, including social media platforms. Images of perfection are everywhere—on TV shows, in movies, in magazines, and all over platforms like Instagram and TikTok. These images often show an unrealistic standard of beauty, which can make you feel like your own body isn't good enough.

Family and Parental Influence

Family attitudes toward body image and appearance also play a significant role. If family members focus heavily on looks or dieting, it might lead you to believe that appearance is tied to worth.

Peers

Your friends and classmates can also influence your body image. Comments, jokes, or even casual remarks about someone's appearance can reinforce negative body image or the importance of looking a certain way.

The Statistics Tell a Story

Body image issues are incredibly common among teens, particularly girls. According to research by the National Organization for Women, by age thirteen, 53 percent of girls are unhappy with their bodies. This dissatisfaction increases as they grow, with up to 78 percent of seventeen-year-old girls feeling unhappy about their appearance. These concerns are not limited to adolescence; many adult women continue to struggle with body image.

The Dangers of Comparison

Comparing yourself to others can exacerbate body image issues. Whether it's someone you see online or a classmate, comparison can steal your joy and damage your self-esteem. Here's why comparisons are harmful:

- **Unfairness**: Comparisons often ignore the differences in opportunities, resources, and personal journeys.
- **Focus on the Wrong Person**: Focusing on others can distract you from your own growth and achievements.
- **Endless Possibilities for Comparison**: There will always be someone to compare yourself to, leading to an endless cycle of dissatisfaction.
- **Loss of Joy:** Seeing only how you "stack up" can make you miss out on celebrating your own unique qualities and achievements.
- **Incomparable Uniqueness**: Trying to compare two people is like comparing apples to zebras—they're just too different. Everyone has unique traits and life experiences that make direct comparisons meaningless.
- **Distorted Self-Image**: When you compare yourself to others, especially without knowing their full story, you risk building a distorted view of yourself. This can lead to feelings of inadequacy or an inflated ego, neither of which reflects your true self.

How to Break the Cycle of Comparison

To combat negative body image and the urge to compare yourself, consider these strategies:

- **Practice Gratitude and Body Kindness**: Appreciate your body for what it can do rather than how it looks. Celebrate its strengths and what it allows you to experience.
- **Identify Triggers**: Be aware of what situations or emotions trigger your comparisons, and try to understand or avoid these triggers.
- **Focus on Your Strengths:** Remind yourself of your talents and achievements that aren't related to appearance.
- **Redirect Thoughts**: Learn to redirect your thoughts when you find yourself making comparisons. Instead, think of how all the things about you make you wonderfully unique.
- **Filter Your Social Media Feed**: Unfollow accounts that make you feel bad about your body or promote unrealistic beauty standards.
- **Celebrate Others' Successes**: Try to feel joy for others' accomplishments rather than jealousy or inadequacy.

Embracing Imperfections

Understanding that imperfections are part of being human can help you accept and embrace your own. Every person has flaws, and it's these flaws that make you unique. Recognizing the beauty in imperfection can transform how you view yourself and others. It's not about having the perfect body but about appreciating your body for what it is and recognizing the beauty in diversity—of shapes, sizes, and colors.

Learning to accept and love yourself just as you are is a powerful antidote to the perfectionism that plagues so many aspects of life. By focusing on health, happiness, and personal growth rather than perfection, you can develop a healthier body image and a more fulfilling life.

INTERACTIVE ELEMENT: BECOMING PERFECTLY IMPERFECT

Perfectionism can be a tough hurdle in your teenage years, especially with all the pressures from school, peers, and social media. Here's a simple, practical activity designed to help you recognize and reduce perfectionistic tendencies. This activity can be done alone or with a group of friends, providing a space for open discussion and self-reflection.

Part 1: Identifying Perfectionistic Traits

Step 1: Recognize Your Perfectionistic Thoughts

Before you can change perfectionistic habits, you need to identify them. Think about the times when you felt you had to be perfect. What were you doing? What were you thinking? Write down these thoughts below:

____

____

____

I feel I must be perfect when:

____

____

____

Step 2: Analyze Your Thoughts

Look at what you've written. How do these thoughts make you feel? Anxious, sad, or maybe frustrated? Write about your feelings here:

____

____

____

These thoughts make me feel:

____

____

____

Part 2: Challenging Perfectionism

Step 3: Challenge Your Perfectionistic Thinking

For each perfectionistic thought you've identified, try to come up with a more realistic and kinder way to think about the situation. Turn "I must not make any mistakes on this test" into "It's okay to make mistakes. I can learn from them." Write your new thoughts here:

___

___

___

Instead of thinking "..." I can think "...":

___

___

___

Part 3: Implementing Changes

Step 4: Plan to Overcome Perfectionism

Now that you've identified and reframed your perfectionistic thoughts, think about specific actions you can take to not let these thoughts control your behavior. For example, if you're worried about an upcoming presentation, instead of obsessing over every detail, you could set a time limit for your preparation and then relax.

___

___

___

What actions can I take to overcome my perfectionism?

____

____

____

Step 5: Reflect on Your Experience

After trying out your new approaches, reflect on how it felt. Were you less stressed? Did you enjoy the activity more, even if it wasn't perfect? Write about your experience here:

Reflecting on my experience, I noticed:

____

____

____

Part 4: Celebrating Progress

Step 6: Reward Yourself

Finally, learn to celebrate your efforts rather than the outcome. Did you give a presentation and manage to stay calm, even if it wasn't perfect? That's a huge success! Think about ways you can reward yourself for trying and improving, not just for achieving perfection.

____

____

____

How Will I Reward Myself for Trying My Best?

This activity is designed to help you see that being perfect isn't necessary to be successful or happy. It's about effort, learning, and growth. Embrace your imperfections, and remember that every step you take toward overcoming perfectionism is a step toward a happier, healthier you.

FINAL THOUGHTS

Throughout this chapter, we have delved deep into the intricacies of perfectionism, particularly how it influences teenagers' self-perception and daily behaviors. We've explored the definitions and manifestations of perfectionism, highlighting how this trait can lead to significant stress and anxiety when young people feel pressured to meet unrealistic standards in various aspects of their lives, from academic achievements to social interactions and physical appearance.

Perfectionism often arises from the belief that one's value is deeply tied to their accomplishments, which can drive teens to strive relentlessly for flawless results. We discussed how such expectations are not only unrealistic but also unhealthy, as they can lead to critical self-assessment, fear of failure, and a distorted body image. Notably, the media and societal expectations can exacerbate these pressures, showcasing idealized images and lifestyles that are often unattainable.

Moreover, the chapter outlined practical strategies to help you recognize and challenge perfectionistic tendencies. Techniques such as adjusting your self-talk, setting realistic goals, and focusing on progress rather than perfection are crucial steps in mitigating the negative impacts of this mindset. We also emphasized the importance of self-compassion and understanding that making mistakes is a natural, important part of learning and personal growth.

Moving forward, the next chapter shifts focus from the external pressures of achieving perfection to the internal values that guide personal conduct, namely integrity and staying true to oneself. Integrity involves being honest and having strong moral principles. It is about making choices that are not only legally right but are also in alignment with your personal values and the truth of who you are.

As we transition from discussing how to let go of perfectionism, it's essential to consider how integrity plays a pivotal role in building a healthy self-concept. While perfectionism often pushes you to mold yourself based on external expectations and approval, integrity calls you to act according to your true self. It's about being the same person on the outside as you are on the inside, regardless of who is watching. This alignment between your actions and your values is foundational to developing a strong sense of self and true self-esteem.

In the next chapter, we will explore various dimensions of integrity, including the courage it takes to be true to oneself in the face of social pressures. We'll discuss how living with integrity impacts relationships, self-respect, and overall life satisfaction. You'll learn how embracing your authentic self can free you from the impossible chase for perfection and allow you to live a more fulfilling and meaningful life.

Additionally, the concept of integrity extends to how you interact with others. Being true to yourself includes expressing your thoughts and feelings honestly and respectfully, which ties back to our discussions on overcoming perfectionism. When you stop trying to be perfect for others and start being genuine for yourself, you can build stronger, more authentic connections.

Ultimately, this journey from striving for perfection to living with integrity is about shifting from a focus on external validation to internal peace. It's about realizing that the truest form of success comes from being honest with yourself and making choices that reflect your values and aspirations. This transition is crucial for personal growth and happiness, and it prepares you for a life led not by the fear of inadequacy but by the confidence of authenticity.

Make a Difference with Your Review

UNLOCK THE POWER OF GENEROSITY

"True happiness comes from helping others."

— *DALAI LAMA*

Did you know that helping others can make you feel happier, live longer, and even be more successful? It's true! And today, I have a small favor to ask that can make a big difference.

Would you help someone you've never met, even if you never got credit for it?

Who is this person, you ask? They are like you. Or, at least, like you used to be. Someone less experienced, wanting to make a difference, and needing help but not sure where to look.

Our mission is to make self-love, self-confidence, and self-esteem accessible to every teen girl. Everything I do stems from that mission. And, the only way for me to accomplish that mission is by reaching. . .well...everyone.

This is where you come in. Most people do, in fact, judge a book by its cover (and its reviews). So here's my ask on behalf of a struggling teen girl you've never met:

Please help those teen girls by leaving this book a review.

Your gift costs no money and less than 60 seconds to make real, but it can change a fellow teen girl's life forever. Your review could help. . .

...one more girl feel confident in her own skin.
...one more girl make a new friend.
...one more girl speak up for herself.
...one more girl achieve her dreams.
...one more girl believe in her worth.

To get that 'feel good' feeling and help this person for real, all you have to do is leave a review.

Simply scan the QR code to leave your review:

If you feel good about helping a faceless teen girl, you are my kind of person. Welcome to the club. You're one of us.

I'm that much more excited to help you build your self-love, self-confidence, and self-esteem faster and easier than you can possibly imagine. You'll love the tools and strategies I'm about to share in the coming chapters.

Thank you from the bottom of my heart. Now, back to our regularly scheduled program.

- Your biggest fan, Lizanne Douglas

PS - Fun fact: If you provide something of value to another person, it makes you more valuable to them. If you'd like goodwill straight from another teen girl - and you believe this book will help them - send this book their way.

S
E
I
F
I-Integrity
E

CHAPTER 6

I—Integrity—Staying True to Yourself—Overcoming People Pleasing

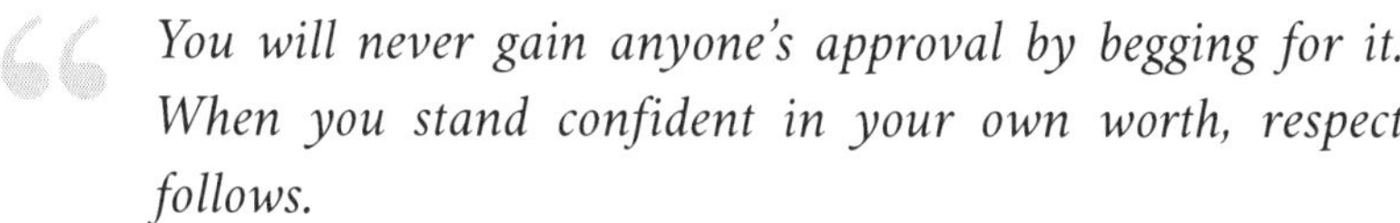

> *You will never gain anyone's approval by begging for it. When you stand confident in your own worth, respect follows.*
>
> — MANDY HALE

Have you ever found yourself saying yes to things you really wanted to say no to? Maybe it's staying late to help a friend with a project, attending a party you're not excited about, or joining a club just because someone asked you to. It's great to be known as a reliable, helpful, and kind person, right? But sometimes, does it feel like you're doing more things for others and less for yourself?

This tug between doing what others expect and what you actually want is a common struggle. It's like being caught in a cycle of wanting to make everyone happy, often at the expense of your own happiness or comfort. This is what people often refer to as people-pleasing behavior.

WHAT IS PEOPLE PLEASING?

It sounds like you're always the go-to person when someone needs a hand with homework or a project. That's awesome—you're seen as helpful and kind, and that's a great quality. But do you sometimes feel like you're stretching yourself too thin for others, often at the expense of your own needs? If that sounds familiar, you might be leaning into people-pleasing behaviors more than you realize.

What Are the Signs of a People Pleaser?

- **Always Agreeing**: It's cool to be the kind of person who listens and is respectful, but if you find yourself agreeing with everything everyone says just to be liked or avoid conflict, it might be a sign of people pleasing. This can leave you feeling like you're not really being true to yourself.
- **Frequent Apologizing**: Do you find yourself saying sorry for things that aren't even your fault? It's one thing to apologize if you've messed up, but if you're constantly taking the blame for other people's emotions or reactions, you might be shouldering too much responsibility.

- **Struggling to Say No:** This is a big one. If saying no feels impossible, and you end up overcommitting and feeling overwhelmed, that's a classic sign of a people pleaser. You might even make up excuses later to get out of plans because saying no upfront feels too hard.
- **Changing Your Personality**: If you act differently depending on who you're with, trying to match their expectations or avoid rocking the boat, it's worth asking yourself if you're doing things that really feel right to you. This can lead to feeling lost or uncertain about who you really are.
- **Seeking Validation**: Do you feel good about yourself mainly when others approve of you? If your self-esteem depends heavily on getting praise from others, it might be time to look inward and start valuing your own opinion of yourself.

THE LINK BETWEEN PEOPLE-PLEASING BEHAVIOR AND LOW SELF-ESTEEM

The link between people-pleasing behavior and low self-esteem is that people pleasing often stems from an underlying need for approval and acceptance. Individuals who consistently put others' needs and desires above their own may do so because they see their worth through the lens of others' perceptions. This reliance on external validation can lead to low self-esteem, as people pleasers may neglect their own needs and base their self-worth on the approval of others, leading to feelings of inadequacy and low self-value.

More about People Pleasing

In a nutshell, people pleasing involves excessive efforts to keep others around you happy, often at your own expense. As mentioned before, it includes agreeing to things you'd rather not do, suppressing your true thoughts and feelings to avoid conflict, and going out of your way to maintain harmony in relationships. This behavior can lead to feelings of being overwhelmed and stressed, as it involves constantly managing others' happiness and avoiding any form of disappointment.

Signs and Symptoms of People-Pleasing Behavior Stemming from Lack of Self- Esteem

Here are some common signs that you might be engaging in people-pleasing behaviors:

- **Difficulty Saying "No":** Struggling to set personal boundaries and fearing the disappointment of others often leads to an inability to refuse requests, even when they are unreasonable or inconvenient.
- **Constant Need for Approval:** Your self-worth might be heavily dependent on the validation and approval of others, leading you to go to great lengths to please everyone around you.
- **Overcommitting**: Regularly taking on more than you can manage because you can't say no, which often leads to personal burnout.
- **Neglecting Personal Needs**: Prioritizing everyone else's needs over your own can result in neglecting your physical, emotional, and mental health.

- **Avoiding Conflict:** You might avoid expressing your true thoughts and feelings if you believe they could cause disagreement or confrontation.
- **Overapologizing**: You find yourself frequently apologizing for things, even when you are not at fault. This behavior stems from a fear of being disliked or blamed and a need to maintain harmony at your own expense.
- **Overcompensating with Gifts or Favors**: To ensure that others view you favorably, you might often go out of your way to do things for them, even if it means inconveniencing yourself. This could include buying gifts excessively or offering help persistently as a means to secure their approval and affection.
- **Discounting Compliments**: When someone compliments you, you struggle to accept it and might deflect or minimize it instead. This behavior indicates a low self-esteem, as you may not believe you truly deserve the praise or feel uncomfortable being the focus of positive attention.
- **Overachieving and Perfectionism**: Driven by a fear of criticism or being average, you might push yourself to achieve flawless results in everything you do. This often leads to setting unrealistically high standards for yourself, which can be mentally and physically exhausting.

Effects of Being a People Pleaser

Constantly trying to please others can lead to a number of negative outcomes, including:

- **Lack of Self-Care:** Always being there for others can mean not being there for yourself. This might manifest as neglecting your own health, interests, or emotional needs, which can lead to burnout.

- **Resentment:** While you may start out with good intentions, over time, always trying to please others can lead to feelings of resentment, especially if you feel taken advantage of.
- **Difficulty Enjoying Life**: With your schedule and mental energy consumed by meeting others' expectations, finding time to relax and enjoy the things you love can become increasingly difficult.

How to Make Space for Yourself

To break the cycle of people pleasing, consider these steps:

- **Monitor Your Behavior:** Start by tracking how often you say yes when you really want to say no. Reflect on how these instances make you feel and why you felt unable to refuse.
- **Identify Triggers**: Recognize situations or individuals that particularly trigger your people-pleasing behavior. Understanding these patterns can help you prepare and respond differently in the future.
- **Set Boundaries:** Learn to set and enforce boundaries that protect your time and energy. It's okay to prioritize your own needs and say no without feeling guilty.
- **Align Actions with Values**: Focus your efforts on activities and commitments that align with your personal values and bring you joy, rather than those that solely seek to appease others.
- **Recognize Your Patterns**: Pay attention to when and why you feel compelled to please others at your expense. Is it in all relationships or just specific ones?

- **Self-Care and Self-Worth**: Invest time in understanding your value that doesn't stem from others' approval. Engage in activities that foster your sense of self-worth and independence.
- **Assertiveness Training**: Develop skills to express your feelings and needs directly and respectfully without fearing how others will react.
- **Seek Professional Help**: Therapy can be an effective way to explore the underlying causes of your people-pleasing behaviors and develop healthier ways of relating to others.

Transitioning from a people pleaser to someone who can comfortably set boundaries and advocate for their own needs doesn't mean you stop helping or caring for others. Instead, it allows you to do so in a way that also respects and honors your own needs and well-being. This balance is essential for long-term happiness and health.

Root Causes of People Pleasing

The root of people pleasing can vary but often includes:

- **Low Self-Esteem:** As discussed, feeling unworthy or inadequate can drive a person to seek constant approval from others to feel validated.
- **Fear of Rejection**: The worry that others will reject or think less of you if you don't meet their needs or expectations.
- **Desire for External Validation**: Believing that your value is tied to how much you can do for others.
- **Learned Behaviors**: Growing up in environments where you were rewarded for putting others first and your needs were often overlooked.

THE SEVEN DEADLY SHOULDS

As discussed, people-pleasing behavior might stem from a deep-seated need for approval and acceptance, often rooted in childhood experiences. While it's born from an understandable desire to connect and belong, this tendency can lead to significant emotional strain. Let's take a look at seven beliefs that many individuals with people-pleasing characteristics share:

1. Other people should appreciate and love me because of all the things I do for them.
2. Other people should always like and approve of me because of how hard I work to please them.
3. Other people should never reject or criticize me because I always try to live up to their desires and expectations.
4. Other people should be kind and caring to me in return because of how well I treat them.
5. Other people should never hurt me or treat me unfairly because I'm so nice to them.
6. Other people should never leave or abandon me because of how much I make them need me.
7. Other people should never be angry with me because I would go to any length to avoid conflict, anger, or confrontation with them.

If you've identified one or more of the above as applicable to you, don't despair. You are one step closer to positive change by walking through the game-changing strategies below.

Embracing Authenticity

As you work through these strategies, remember that changing deeply ingrained behaviors takes time and patience. The goal is not to swing from one extreme to the other but to find a balanced way of interacting with the world that respects both your needs and those of others. Embracing your authenticity involves recognizing that you can be kind and supportive without sacrificing your own well-being. It's about being honest with yourself and those around you, making decisions that reflect your true self, and standing by them even when they're unpopular or difficult. This transition is crucial for those who have struggled with people pleasing because it shifts the focus from external validation to internal satisfaction and self-respect.

In our fast-paced world, where doing more often feels like a necessity, it's easy to fall into the trap of people pleasing. It might start as a small "yes" here and there, but over time, this can evolve into a chronic state where your days are spent juggling the demands of others, leaving little room for your own needs and aspirations. If you find yourself constantly trying to meet everyone's expectations at the expense of your well-being, it's crucial to step back and reassess your approach to interpersonal relationships.

Understanding People Pleasing

People-pleasing isn't just about being kind; it's a deeper, more complex behavior rooted in the desire for approval and fear of rejection. While it can make you feel valued in the short term, this behavior often leads to stress, burnout, and a loss of personal identity.

Long-Term and Deep-Rooted Problems of People Pleasing

We've gone over some of the traits of people pleasers and their effects as well. Left unchanged, here are some more serious, deep-rooted issues that can arise:

- **Emotional Overspending**: Frequently feeling overwhelmed or stressed because you've committed to more than you can manage.
- **Resentment under the Surface**: While appearing cheerful and agreeable, you might secretly feel resentful toward those you're trying to please because it often feels one-sided.
- **Passive-Aggressive Behavior**: Occasionally, your true feelings might slip out in passive-aggressive comments, a sign of unaddressed discontent.
- **Self-Neglect:** Regularly putting others' needs before your own, to the point where your own health and well-being suffer.

Steps to Reduce People Pleasing

Breaking free from the people-pleasing cycle involves several actionable steps that focus on self-awareness, boundary setting, and self-respect:

- **Realize You Have a Choice:** Recognition is the first step. Understand that you are not obligated to say yes and that your value does not depend on how much you do for others.

- **Identify Your Priorities:** Determine what truly matters to you. What are your personal and professional goals? Aligning your actions with your priorities makes it easier to make decisions that are right for you.
- **Set Clear Boundaries:** Communicate your limits to others. Boundaries are a healthy way to protect your energy and time.
- **Practice Saying No**: Start small if you need to. Refuse extra commitments that don't align with your priorities or that you genuinely don't have time for.
- **Reflect on Manipulation**: Be aware of situations where you might be manipulated into agreeing. Recognize flattery or guilt-tripping and assess whether someone is genuinely seeking help or merely taking advantage of your accommodating nature.
- **Use Mantra:** Reinforce your resolve with affirmations that remind you of your right to say no and prioritize your well-being.
- **Be Specific:** When agreeing to requests, define how much time you can commit. This prevents open-ended commitments that can lead to burnout.
- **Say No with Conviction**: Develop the ability to say no firmly and respectfully. Prepare phrases such as "I'll need to check my schedule; I'll get back to you" to give yourself time to decide without pressure.
- **Start with Small Noes**: Begin by declining smaller, less consequential requests to build your confidence. This practice helps you prepare for turning down bigger demands.
- **It's Perfectly Fine to Be Imperfect**: Allow yourself to feel uncomfortable when saying no. This discomfort is natural, and it lessens as you grow accustomed to setting boundaries.

- **Keep It Simple**: When you decide to say no, keep your explanation simple and direct. This prevents others from trying to negotiate your boundaries.
- **Don't Apologize—If It's Not Your Fault**: Avoid using apologies when setting boundaries unless you genuinely have something to apologize for. This strengthens your assertiveness and confidence.
- **Fold in Positive Self-Talk**: Encourage yourself with positive statements that boost your self-esteem and reinforce your decisions, such as "I am making the best choice for my well-being."
- **Aim for Progress, Not Perfection**: Take time to recognize and celebrate the steps you've taken toward becoming less of a people pleaser. This reinforces positive behavior and boosts your morale.
- **Monitor Your Behavior:** Start by tracking how often you say yes when you really want to say no. Reflect on how these instances make you feel and why you feel unable to refuse.
- **Identify Triggers**: Recognize situations or individuals that particularly trigger your people-pleasing behavior. Understanding these patterns can help you prepare and respond differently in the future.
- **Align Actions with Values**: Focus your efforts on activities and commitments that align with your personal values and bring you joy, rather than those that solely seek to appease others.
- **Recognize Your Patterns**: Pay attention to when and why you feel compelled to please others at your expense. Is it in all relationships or just specific ones?
- **Establish Boundaries**: Learn to say no and set limits on what you will and will not do. Practice expressing your needs and desires.

- **Self-Care and Self-Worth:** Invest time in understanding your value that doesn't stem from others' approval. Engage in activities that foster your sense of self-worth and independence.
- **Assertiveness Training**: Develop skills to express your feelings and needs directly and respectfully without fearing how others will react.
- **Seek Professional Help:** Therapy can be an effective way to explore the underlying causes of your people-pleasing behaviors and develop healthier ways of relating to others.

Embracing Genuine Self-Expression

As you work through these steps, it's crucial to foster a mindset that values genuine self-expression over conformity. Learning to accept and love your true self, imperfections and all, is key to overcoming the need to please everyone. This change not only benefits your mental health but also leads to more authentic and fulfilling relationships.

By understanding and addressing people-pleasing behaviors, you pave the way for a life where you can make decisions based on what's best for you, not just what will keep others happy. This shift is crucial for personal growth and true emotional well-being.

Embracing a Healthier Approach

As you begin to implement these changes, you may notice shifts in your relationships. Some people may not appreciate your new boundaries, which is a sign of relationships that were benefiting disproportionately from your people pleasing. On the other hand, genuine relationships will strengthen as you interact more authentically.

DEALING WITH PEER PRESSURE

Finding your way through adolescence often involves confronting various social challenges, one of the most pervasive being peer pressure. Understanding this phenomenon, its effects, and strategies for coping with it is crucial for maintaining self-esteem and personal integrity.

What Is Peer Pressure?

Peer pressure is the influence exerted by a peer group in encouraging a person to change their attitudes, values, or behaviors to conform to group norms. During adolescence, the desire for acceptance and fear of rejection are particularly strong, making teens more susceptible to peer influence. This can manifest in various forms, from subtle suggestions about what to wear to more overt coercion regarding risky behaviors like experimenting with drugs or alcohol.

People Pleasing and Peer Pressure

For teens who struggle with people-pleasing behaviors, the impact of peer pressure can be particularly profound. People pleasers often have an acute need for approval and fear of disappointing others, which can make them more likely to succumb to peer pressure. This vulnerability arises because saying no could lead to conflict or rejection, scenarios that people pleasers typically go to great lengths to avoid.

Effects of Peer Pressure

Peer pressure can have both positive and negative effects. On the positive side, peer influence can encourage teens to strive for good grades or join beneficial social activities. However, the negative impacts often overshadow these benefits, leading to stress, anxiety, and engagement in unhealthy behaviors. The stress of constantly trying to conform can also exacerbate feelings of inadequacy and contribute to a distorted sense of self.

The Role of Self-Confidence

Self-confidence is a critical shield against the negative effects of peer pressure. Teens who feel secure in their identities and values are less likely to seek validation by conforming to the detrimental demands of their peer group. Instead, they are more likely to make independent decisions and choose friends who respect their boundaries and values.

Strategies to Handle Peer Pressure

Here are several effective strategies for dealing with peer pressure:

- **Recognize the Signs**: Understanding when you're being pressured can help you prepare to respond.
- **Trust Your Gut:** If something feels off, it probably is. Listening to your intuition can help you stay true to your values.
- **Know Your No:** Prepare a few ways to say no respectfully but firmly. Rehearsing these can make it easier when the moment comes.
- **Choose Your Friends Wisely**: Surround yourself with peers who respect you and your choices.

- **Seek Support:** Talk to trusted adults or friends who are not part of the immediate peer group exerting pressure.

SETTING BOUNDARIES

Why Boundaries Are Important

Setting boundaries is crucial, not only for dealing with peer pressure but for all aspects of a teen's life. Boundaries help define what you are comfortable with and how you expect to be treated by others. They are essential for:

- **Safety and Security**: Protecting both physical and emotional well-being.
- **Personal Responsibility**: Encouraging independence and accountability.
- **Healthy Relationships:** Ensuring mutual respect and appropriate behavior.
- **Emotional Well-Being**: Preventing burnout and resentment.

Types of Boundaries

There are four main types of boundaries. They include:

- **Physical Boundaries:** Respect for personal space and physical touch.
- **Emotional Boundaries**: Protecting emotional health by not absorbing the emotions of others.
- **Social Boundaries**: Limiting social interaction to prevent overcommitment.

- **Time Boundaries:** Allocating time for various activities without overextending.

Boundary Principles

Understanding and setting boundaries is a crucial skill for personal development and maintaining healthy relationships. It empowers individuals to respect themselves and others, fostering mutual respect in various interactions. Here are some foundational boundary principles:

- **We Each Belong to Ourselves**: This principle underscores the idea that every individual has control over their own body, feelings, and choices. It is fundamental to understand that you have the right to your thoughts, feelings, and personal space, and this right should be respected by others, just as you should respect theirs.
- **Some Things Are Not a Choice**: Certain situations require setting nonnegotiable boundaries for your safety and well-being. For example, health and safety rules at home or in school are not choices but requirements that ensure everyone's well-being and must be adhered to.
- **Problems Should Not Be Secrets:** It's important to communicate openly about problems, especially if they affect your safety or emotional health. Keeping problems hidden can prevent you from getting the help you need. If you are struggling, speak up and seek support from trusted adults or peers.
- **Keep Telling until You Get Help**: If your initial attempts to address a problem or set a boundary are not respected, continue to seek help until you find someone who listens and takes action. Persistence is key in situations where your boundaries are not being respected.

How to Set Boundaries

Setting boundaries is a skill that can be developed over time through practice and reflection. Here's how you can start:

- **Identify Your Feelings**: Intuition is a powerful guide. If something feels off, it probably is. Trusting your gut helps in recognizing when boundaries are being crossed, even if you might not have an immediate explanation for why you feel a certain way.
- **Identify Unacceptable Behaviors**: Determine behaviors you find unacceptable and communicate these clearly to others. For instance, if you are not comfortable with someone borrowing your belongings without asking, that's a boundary you should communicate.

- **Examples of Healthy Boundaries**:

    - Saying no to things you're not comfortable with without feeling guilty.
    - Asking for personal space when needed.

- **Examples of Unhealthy Boundaries**

    - Letting people pressure you into doing things you don't want to.
    - Not expressing when you're uncomfortable due to fear of others' reactions.

- **Understand the Importance of Digital Boundaries**: Digital boundaries are equally important as physical ones. This includes privacy settings on social media, deciding

who gets to see your posts, and how much time you spend online.
- **Use Key Phrases to Diffuse Situations**: Phrases like "I'm not comfortable with this" or "Please respect my privacy" are helpful. Practice saying these out loud so you can be prepared to use them when needed.
- **Practice at Home**: Begin setting boundaries in a safe environment like home. Practice expressing your needs and limits clearly to family members.
- **Understand That Friendships Have Limits**: Every relationship has limits; understanding these can prevent feelings of betrayal or disappointment. Communicate openly about what you are and aren't capable of in friendships.
- **Respect the Boundaries of Others**: Just as you expect others to respect your boundaries, it's important to respect theirs. This reciprocal understanding is crucial for healthy relationships.

Communicating Boundaries

Effectively communicating your boundaries involves clear, assertive communication. Here's how you might articulate them across different relationships:

- **To a Parent**: "I appreciate your advice, but I need to handle this situation on my own to learn from it."
- **To a Teacher or Coach**: "I value your feedback, but I feel overwhelmed. Can we discuss a more manageable approach?"
- **To a Friend**: "I'm not comfortable with that. Let's do something else instead."

- **To a Date:** "I like spending time with you, but I need to go home by 9 PM."

Common Reactions to Boundaries

When you begin to set and enforce boundaries, it's not uncommon to encounter resistance. People who are used to a certain dynamic might react negatively when you start to assert your needs. Understanding these reactions can help you prepare and stay firm in your position. Here are some typical responses you might encounter:

- **Denial**: Some individuals may outright deny that your boundaries are necessary or valid. They might insist that the issues you're raising aren't real or important, suggesting that you're overreacting or misinterpreting the situation.
- **Minimizing**: This reaction involves downplaying your feelings or the need for boundaries. Someone might acknowledge your boundary but trivialize it, suggesting that it's not as crucial as you think or that you're making a big deal out of nothing.
- **Counterattacking with Emotional Coercion:** In some cases, individuals might respond to your boundaries by trying to manipulate your emotions. This can include:
- **Guilt:** Making you feel guilty for even suggesting a boundary, implying that your needs are selfish or unreasonable.
- **Blame:** Shifting the blame onto you, suggesting that any problems are your fault, not a result of their actions.
- **Putting Words in Your Mouth**: Misrepresenting what you've said to make it seem as though you're being unreasonable or hurtful.

- **Denying Your Right to Have a Boundary**: Some may refuse to acknowledge your right to set any boundaries at all. They might assert that, as a friend, family member, or partner, you should not have such restrictions in your relationship, implying that your desire for boundaries is an indictment of the relationship itself.
- **Being So Devastated That You Feel Tempted to Take Care of Him or Her**: Another common reaction is for the person to act so hurt or devastated by your boundaries that you feel compelled to revert to old patterns just to comfort them. This can be a powerful form of manipulation, as it plays directly on your sympathies and can make you feel responsible for their emotional well-being.

Recognizing these reactions for what they are—responses to changes in relationship dynamics—can help you maintain your resolve. It's important to stay firm in your boundaries despite these reactions, as they are often tests to see if you will revert to old behaviors. Consistency is key to showing that you are serious about your needs and that your boundaries are not up for negotiation.

Responding to Boundary Pushback

Not everyone will respect your boundaries the first time. You might encounter denial, minimization, or even emotional coercion. Here are steps to maintain your stance:

- **Acknowledge Feelings:** Recognize the other person's feelings without compromising your own boundaries.

- **Express Caring While Restating Your Boundary**: "I care about our friendship, but I need to stick to what's right for me."
- **Find Common Ground:** Identify areas where you can agree without giving in.
- **State Realistic Consequences**: Be clear about what will happen if your boundaries are continuously ignored.
- **Take a Break and Try Again Later:** If the conversation becomes too heated or unproductive, suggest pausing the discussion and revisiting it when both parties are calmer.
- **Leave Quietly and Get Help:** If you feel unsafe or if the situation escalates beyond your control, it's important to leave the environment and seek assistance from someone you trust.
- **Request Clarification:** If responses to your boundaries are vague or confusing, ask for clarification to ensure there is no misunderstanding about what is being communicated.
- **Write It Down:** Sometimes, writing down your boundaries can help others understand them more clearly. This can be especially effective in professional settings or when dealing with complex issues.
- **As a Last Resort, Know When and How to Use Physical Self-Defense:** In situations where your physical safety is threatened, knowing basic self-defense techniques can be vital. Only use this as a last resort when all other options have been exhausted.

Adolescence is a formative period where you lay the groundwork for the adult you will become. By understanding and managing peer pressure and setting and enforcing boundaries, you equip yourself with the tools to build a healthy, autonomous, and fulfilling life. As we close this chapter, we move into discussions on enrichment and how to attain a growth mindset.

INTERACTIVE ELEMENT: OVERCOMING PEOPLE PLEASING AND FINDING HAPPINESS WITHIN

Reflecting on how you engage with the world and others can provide valuable insights into your habitual behaviors, especially those shaped early in your life. This activity is designed to help you understand the roots of your people-pleasing tendencies and guide you toward a more self-directed and authentic expression of yourself.

Think back to an instance from your early childhood (between the ages of two and ten) where you felt criticized or wrong for simply being yourself. For instance, perhaps you were being playful and loud and were scolded, being told to "act grown-up."

Describe the Incident

____

____

____

How did you feel during that moment? (E.g., sad, angry, ashamed.)

____

____

____

In response to this situation, what aspects of your true self did you feel you had to suppress?

____

____

____

Who did you decide you needed to become to avoid the pain of rejection and ensure you were loved and accepted?

____

____

____

Exploring Your Reactions to Approval and Praise

What emotional or other personal gains do you experience when someone approves of or praises you? How do you react when you do not receive approval?

Are there specific individuals whose acceptance and approval you particularly seek? Why do you think their approval matters so much to you?

Reflect on the impact of your pursuit of approval on your life. What are you missing out on because of this pursuit?

____

____

____

Envision a new way of being that feels more true to who you really are. What changes would you like to make? How can you begin to adopt this new approach to life?

____

____

____

____

____

This exercise helps you explore the origins of your people-pleasing behavior, connecting past experiences to current patterns, and encourages you to envision a shift toward authenticity and self-expression.

FINAL THOUGHTS

In this chapter, we learned about the complexities of people-pleasing behavior, uncovering its roots, manifestations, and the deep-seated reasons why some individuals continually prioritize the happiness of others over their own needs. This exploration has brought to light how people pleasing is not merely a superficial tendency to be nice but is often a profound psychological response rooted in early life experiences.

From a young age, many people pleasers learn that their value is contingent upon the approval and happiness of others. This can stem from childhood environments where the love and attention of caregivers were conditional upon the child's behavior, leading them to adopt a pleasing persona to secure affection and avoid conflict. As these individuals grow, the pattern becomes ingrained and extends into various aspects of their lives, including friendships, romantic relationships, and professional environments.

One of the critical insights from this chapter is recognizing the signs of people-pleasing behavior. These signs include an inability to say no, a tendency to agree with others, even when disagreeing internally, and a habit of overapologizing and changing one's personality to match others' expectations. Such behaviors are driven by a deep fear of rejection and a strong desire for acceptance, which often leads to neglecting one's own needs and desires.

The emotional toll of people pleasing is significant. Constantly striving to meet others' expectations can lead to stress, burnout, and a loss of personal identity. People pleasers often find themselves in a paradox where their efforts to make others happy lead to personal unhappiness and resentment. This cycle can be hard to break, as it is fueled by the fear that not pleasing others will result in disapproval and abandonment.

Addressing people-pleasing behavior involves several transformative steps, the first of which is awareness. Recognizing the patterns and understanding their origins is crucial in beginning to make changes. This chapter emphasizes the importance of setting boundaries as a practical approach to reducing people-pleasing tendencies. Establishing what behaviors are acceptable and what aren't helps in defining one's limits and expectations, both for oneself and in relation to others.

Setting boundaries is an act of self-care and self-respect. It involves understanding and articulating one's needs and limits and standing by them even when pressured by others. This can be challenging for a people pleaser, as it requires facing the discomfort of potentially upsetting others. However, the act of setting boundaries is crucial for emotional well-being and the development of healthy, balanced relationships.

Another significant aspect of reducing people-pleasing behavior is learning to value oneself independently of others' opinions and approval. This involves cultivating self-esteem and confidence, which enables individuals to make decisions based on their values and preferences rather than external validation. It also includes embracing imperfections and understanding that making mistakes does not diminish one's worth.

Communication plays a pivotal role in managing people-pleasing tendencies. Effectively communicating one's feelings and needs without fear of conflict can transform relationships and personal well-being. It encourages honesty and openness, which are foundational to genuine connections and respect between individuals.

The chapter also addressed the nuanced nature of people pleasing, pointing out that while it is often viewed negatively, the qualities that underpin this behavior—empathy, sensitivity, and thoughtfulness—are inherently positive. The goal is not to eradicate these qualities but to balance them with self-respect and self-care. This balance ensures that acts of kindness and cooperation are choices that enhance relationships rather than sacrifices that diminish one's sense of self.

In summary, moving away from people pleasing is not about becoming less caring or cooperative but about developing a stronger sense of self that allows for caring for others without losing oneself in the process. It's about establishing a life where personal needs are met with the same enthusiasm with which one meets the needs of others. This shift not only enhances personal growth and happiness but also leads to more authentic and fulfilling relationships.

As we wrap up this chapter, we get ready to transition into the next topic, which focuses on cultivating growth. Understanding and overcoming people pleasing is just one part of a broader journey toward personal development, and the next chapter will explore how to foster a mindset that embraces growth, resilience, and true self-expression. This natural progression from recognizing and addressing limiting behaviors sets the stage for nurturing a fulfilling and happy life.

E-Enrichment
S
E
L
F
I

CHAPTER 7

E—Enrichment—Cultivating a Growth Mindset—Building Your Path to Success

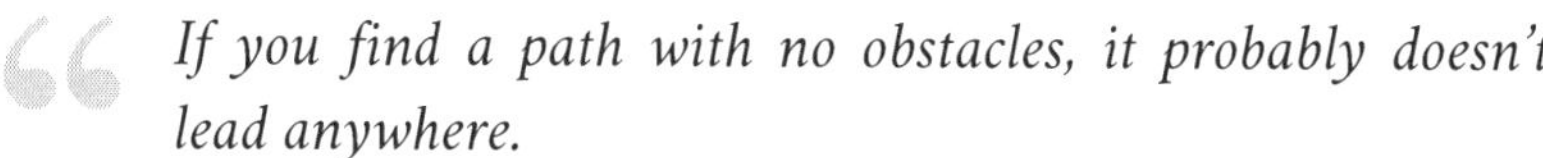

> *If you find a path with no obstacles, it probably doesn't lead anywhere.*
>
> — FRANK A. CLARK

WHAT IS A GROWTH MINDSET?

Have you ever discovered something so game-changing that it completely shifts how you see yourself and the world around you? That's exactly what the concept of "growth mindset" is all about.

Imagine this: You're learning a new language, and it feels like hitting a brick wall. You might think, "I'm just not good at this." But what if you shifted your perspective to "Maybe I need to try a different way to learn this"? That's a growth mindset in action—it's about believing that with effort and strategy, you can improve.

Think about a time when you felt like giving up on something because it was too hard. Maybe it was a drawing, a math problem, or even a sport. If you had known about the growth mindset, you might have thought, "I'm not where I want to be yet, but I can get better if I keep practicing."

A growth mindset is a concept created by Carol Dweck, a professor at Stanford. Her research shows that people who believe their abilities can be developed (through hard work, strategies, and help from others) are more successful. They see challenges as chances to grow rather than signs of failure.

Growth vs. Fixed Mindset

With a fixed mindset, people believe their qualities are set in stone—you either have it or you don't. This can stop you from trying new things because you're scared of looking bad if you fail. But with a growth mindset, you see yourself as a work in progress. Effort is what helps you build your abilities, like muscles getting stronger the more you use them.

Why Embrace a Growth Mindset?

Adopting a growth mindset can make a huge difference. Let's say you're struggling with those verb conjugations in French. Instead of feeling stuck, you see each mistake as a clue on how to get better. Your motto becomes "Not yet" instead of "I can't."

Or if you've ever felt you're terrible at drawing, adopting a growth mindset means you keep practicing, learning from each sketch, and gradually getting better. The focus is on improvement, not perfection.

Tips for Developing a Growth Mindset

If you want to develop a growth mindset, here are some pointers:

- **Value Effort over Perfection:** Cheer yourself on for the hard work, not just the final results. Acknowledge your effort as the path to mastering new skills.
- **Learn from Setbacks:** Instead of getting down about what went wrong, use mistakes as learning opportunities. What can they teach you?
- **Reflect on Your Learning:** Take time to think about what you've learned from each experience. How have you improved? What strategies worked?
- **Think Critically and Solve Problems:** Encourage yourself to come up with your own solutions instead of waiting for others to fix things. This builds your independence and problem-solving skills.
- **Be Your Own Role Model:** Share your challenges and how you've overcome them. Be the example of a growth mindset to inspire others.

By seeing every challenge as a chance to grow, you unlock a world where learning is exciting and possibilities are endless. So, next time you're faced with something tough, remember that it's not about whether you can do it right now—it's about how you can learn to do it better.

HOW A GROWTH MINDSET RELATES TO SELF-ESTEEM AND SELF-CONFIDENCE

Having a growth mindset can really boost your confidence and cut down on stress. It's all about believing that you can improve through effort and persistence. When you think this way, you're more open to trying new things and not as scared of messing up. This is crucial because every time you step out of your comfort zone, you're learning and growing, even if things don't go perfectly.

Here Is a Simple Breakdown of Growth vs. Fixed Mindset

- **Fixed Mindset**: You might think that your abilities are set in stone. If you believe you're either "good" or "bad" at something and that can't change, this is a fixed mindset.
- **Growth Mindset:** This is when you believe you can get better at something with effort and time. It's about thinking, "I might not be great at this now, but I can improve with practice."

Having a growth mindset can make a huge difference when you're facing challenges. For example, if you struggle with a subject at school, instead of thinking you're just bad at it, a growth mindset helps you see this as a chance to dive in and get better. This approach reduces anxiety because you're not constantly worried about proving yourself. Instead, you're focused on growing and learning, which naturally builds your confidence.

The Power of Your Brain

Neuroscience shows that our brains change and develop when we learn new things. So every time you learn a new skill, whether it's playing a guitar or solving math problems, your brain is getting stronger and making new connections. This is a real, physical change that happens in your brain, which shows you can actually see growth and improvement.

What You Can Do

Changing from a fixed mindset to a growth mindset isn't just helpful for school—it's something that can positively impact every part of your life. It helps you deal with ups and downs more smoothly and keeps you pushing toward your goals. Plus, it's never too late to start thinking this way. Whether you're dealing with school stress or just trying to learn a new hobby, adopting a growth mindset can open the door to new possibilities and a more confident you.

Overcoming Fears and Insecurities by Having a Growth Mindset

Sometimes it feels like we're not all that great, especially during those awkward teen years. Maybe you feel a bit out of shape, or your hair isn't how you like it, or you have some skin issues. We all have something about ourselves that feels less than perfect.

Often, we get caught up in these feelings because we're worried about what others might think. Like, maybe you feel bad about your weight. But why? Often, it's because you think looking a certain way will make you more likable or get more attention, which, deep down, might be about wanting to feel less lonely or more accepted.

But here's the thing: Growing isn't just about shedding a few pounds or fixing what's on the outside. It's about changing how we see these challenges—not as dead ends but as opportunities to become stronger, smarter, and more resilient.

Let's be real: Having a growth mindset doesn't mean ignoring the negatives. Sure, you might feel down about having bad teeth, but rather than dwell on it, you'd think about the next steps, like seeing a dentist. It's about handling what you can and not stressing too much about the outcomes. After all, in the grand scheme of things, most setbacks aren't as catastrophic as they seem at the moment.

Seeing failure as an opportunity is a key part of a growth mindset. Perfection doesn't exist, and that's good because it means there's always room to improve. If you mess up or if something isn't going right, that's your chance to make it better. And if it can't be fixed? Well, sometimes it's okay to let things go and move on.

In life, we're all a little flawed—that's just part of being human. But instead of getting hung up on these flaws, why not look at them differently? They aren't necessarily bad; they just are. And how you choose to handle them can turn them into something positive.

So, we're not perfect, and neither are you, and that's totally fine. We're all in this together, figuring it out one step at a time. And remember, nobody's going to break your stride. You've got this—just keep moving forward.

If you think your intelligence, talent, and other qualities are just built in and can't change, that's called a fixed mindset. This mindset might make you believe that if you're not good at something now, you'll never be good at it. On the other hand, a growth mindset is the belief that you can develop your intelligence and talents with time, practice, and effort. This mindset greatly influences your motivation, resilience, and success.

Understanding these concepts is one thing but applying them in real life can sometimes be confusing. How do you switch from a fixed to a growth mindset? How can you talk about these ideas in ways that really stick, especially for young people?

Taking what we've learned so far and putting it into action, let's break down some scenarios to see the difference between a fixed and growth mindset in action, focusing on identity, self-improvement, comparing yourself to others, and learning new things:

Identity and Self-Improvement

Fixed Mindset: You might think, "I'm either good at something or I'm not."

Growth Mindset: Instead, think, "I can always improve my skills with effort and practice."

For example, maybe you've always told yourself you're not an athletic person. With a growth mindset, you'd start to see sports as a skill you can develop rather than something you're inherently bad at. Getting better might involve extra practice, asking for help, or finding new ways to learn. It may also mean choosing one sport that is easier or more fun for you than the rest.

Comparing to Others

Mindset: It's easy to feel down when others do well, thinking, "It's not fair. They're just naturally smart or talented."

Growth Mindset: Instead, you might think, "Their success shows what's possible. How did they achieve it? What can I learn from them?"

This shift is crucial when you feel jealous or inferior. Remembering that everyone starts somewhere and improves through effort can change how you view others' achievements—from sources of envy to sources of inspiration.

Learning Something New

Fixed Mindset: The fear of making mistakes might hold you back, leading you to think, "If I don't try, I won't fail."

Growth Mindset: Embrace challenges by thinking, "I need to try new and difficult things to grow, even if I fail at first."

For instance, if you're learning to play the guitar and find it tough, a growth mindset would help you see each mistake as a step toward mastering chords and songs, not as a reason to give up.

These examples review how adopting a growth mindset can change your approach to learning and personal growth. Instead of seeing limits, you start to see opportunities. The key is to consciously choose how you interpret challenges, feedback, and even your own talents. This way, you not only improve but also begin to enjoy the journey of learning itself.

Added Benefits of Having a Growth Mindset

Embracing a growth mindset has tremendous advantages for students, as highlighted by Carol Dweck. This mindset encourages the belief that abilities can be developed through effort and learning, unlike a fixed mindset, which views talents as innate and unchangeable.

- **Better Learning Habits**: With a growth mindset, you realize that intelligence isn't fixed, encouraging a proactive approach to learning. This mindset emphasizes the importance of effort and sees improvement as a result of dedication, transforming how you engage with your studies and face new challenges.
- **Boosts Creativity and Innovation:** Innovation isn't reserved for top students alone. Many influential figures weren't academic stars but succeeded through creativity and perseverance. A growth mindset motivates you to think outside the box and explore unconventional ideas and paths.
- **Readiness to Tackle Challenges**: Life is full of obstacles, and a growth mindset equips you to face and overcome these hurdles. It teaches you to perceive challenges as opportunities for personal growth, enhancing your adaptability and resilience.
- **Fosters Healthy Competition**: Seen through the lens of a growth mindset, competition becomes a driving force for self-improvement rather than a battle for superiority. This perspective encourages striving for personal bests rather than comparing oneself to others.
- **Enhances Flexibility**: In today's fast-evolving world, flexibility is key. Students with a growth mindset thrive amid cultural, technological, and global shifts, adapting to new challenges and persevering through difficulties.
- **Sets the Stage for Career Success**: Future careers will demand a diverse set of skills, particularly digital ones. By encouraging you to set clear goals, like SMART goals, a growth mindset prepares you for success, building essential qualities such as self-motivation and confidence.

- **Supports Emotional and Mental Well-Being**: Adopting a growth mindset can significantly impact your emotional health, helping you manage stress and maintain higher levels of happiness. This outlook enables you to better navigate the complexities of both student and professional life, fostering a resilient and positive mental state.

Developing a growth mindset as a teenager not only enhances academic and personal growth but also sets the foundation for a resilient and fulfilling life. It's about seeing potential where others see limitations and continuously seeking improvement.

How to Promote a Growth Mindset

Developing a growth mindset is a transformative journey that involves recognizing and overcoming the limitations of a fixed mindset while embracing principles that foster personal growth and resilience. Let's dive deeper into how you can cultivate a growth mindset and effectively handle criticism, which is an integral part of this development.

Developing a Growth Mindset

- **Recognize Fixed Mindset Traps**: Begin by identifying thoughts that uphold a fixed mindset. These might include beliefs like "I'm just not good at this" or "I can't change." Awareness of these thoughts is the first step toward changing them. When you catch yourself thinking this way, challenge these beliefs and remind yourself that abilities can be developed with time and effort.
- **Embrace Challenges:** Seeing challenges as opportunities rather than obstacles is central to a growth mindset. When faced with a tough task, instead of avoiding it, engage with

it fully, understanding that each challenge is a chance to expand your abilities and learn something new. The more you confront and overcome challenges, the more you will grow.

- **Don't Fear Failure**: Fear of failure can paralyze you, preventing growth. Shift your perspective to see failure as a stepping stone to success. Each failure provides valuable lessons that are vital for learning. Instead of feeling defeated by setbacks, analyze what went wrong and use that knowledge to improve your next attempt.
- **Value Effort over Outcome:** While outcomes are important, focusing solely on results can be discouraging, especially if they don't come immediately. Value the effort and dedication you put into your endeavors. Celebrate the work you do, as effort is a more reliable measure of success than fleeting outcomes.
- **Continue to Learn:** Always seek to expand your knowledge and skills. This could mean reading books, taking courses, or simply exploring new hobbies. Learning keeps your mind active and adaptable, which are key aspects of a growth mindset.
- **Cultivate Persistence**: Persistence is the ability to keep going despite challenges and setbacks. This tenacity is what separates those who achieve their goals from those who fall short. Cultivate persistence by setting small, manageable goals and committing to achieving them, regardless of the difficulties that arise.
- **Seek Out Constructive Feedback:** Feedback is essential for growth. It provides new perspectives on your performance, highlighting areas for improvement that you might not see yourself. Seek out feedback actively, listen to it carefully, and apply it constructively.

Handling Criticism

Handling criticism positively is crucial for maintaining a growth mindset. Here's how to do it effectively:

- **Pause before Reacting:** When you receive criticism, it's natural to react defensively or feel upset. Instead, take a moment to pause and breathe. This helps you respond more thoughtfully and less emotionally.
- **Turn Negatives into Positives**: Try to view criticism as a tool for learning, not an attack. Each piece of feedback is an opportunity to improve. Ask yourself, "What can I learn from this?" This reframes the experience as a positive, even if the feedback itself isn't entirely positive.
- **Everyone Gets Criticized:** Remember, you're not alone in receiving criticism—everyone faces it. Recognizing this can diminish the sting of critical comments and help you take them in stride.
- **Don't Take It Personally**: Try to detach your personal feelings from the feedback. Often, criticism is not about you as a person but about your work or behavior, which you can change and improve.
- **See It as an Avenue for Growth:** Embrace criticism as a part of your growth process. Each critique is a chance to make progress and evolve.
- **Not Every Criticism Is Relevant:** It's important to discern which feedback is useful and which isn't. Not all criticism will be applicable or constructive. Evaluate feedback critically, and apply only what serves your growth.
- **Thank the Critic:** Showing gratitude for feedback can transform a potentially negative interaction into a positive one. It shows maturity and openness to learning.

- **Learn from Criticism**: After receiving feedback, take actionable steps to implement it. This might involve changing how you approach tasks or altering specific behaviors.
- **Be the Better Person**: When you are confident in your own beliefs, you don't feel you have to win an argument or have another person's favor. You are able to be the better person by taking criticism to evaluate and make changes when due and just letting it roll off your back if they are not legitimate.

Building a Supportive Environment

- **Surround Yourself with Growth-Minded People**: The people around you influence your mindset. Surround yourself with individuals who embody the growth mindset principles you aspire to. Their attitudes and behaviors can inspire and motivate you.
- **Celebrate Small Wins and the Success of Others:** Recognizing and celebrating small achievements keeps you motivated. Additionally, celebrating the successes of others encourages a positive, supportive culture that's essential for a growth mindset.

By integrating these practices into your daily life, you can develop an outstanding growth mindset that not only enhances your personal and academic growth but also prepares you for a successful and resilient future.

INTERACTIVE ELEMENT: WHERE THE RUBBER HITS THE ROAD

From Fixed to Growth: Reframing Your Mindset

Understanding the difference between a fixed mindset and a growth mindset is the first step toward personal growth. As mentioned, a fixed mindset holds that our skills and abilities are static and unchangeable, leading to avoidance of challenges and fear of failure. In contrast, a growth mindset embraces challenges as opportunities for development, believing that abilities can improve with effort and perseverance. Use this worksheet to practice shifting your mindset.

Instructions

Below are several statements reflecting a fixed mindset. For each statement, write a response that reflects a growth mindset, focusing on potential, effort, and learning. Use the lines provided to articulate your thoughts fully.

Section 1: Challenges and Effort

Fixed Mindset Statement 1:

"I don't want to try because I'm not naturally good at it."

Your Growth Mindset Response:

____

____

____

Fixed Mindset Statement 2:

"This is way too hard, so it's not worth doing."

Your Growth Mindset Response:

___

___

___

Fixed Mindset Statement 3:

"I made a mistake, so I must not be good at this."

Your Growth Mindset Response:

___

___

___

Section 2: Skills and Abilities

Fixed Mindset Statement 4:

"It's not my fault if I don't have the talent."

Your Growth Mindset Response:

____

____

____

Fixed Mindset Statement 5:

"I'm just not smart enough for this subject."

Your Growth Mindset Response:

____

____

____

Fixed Mindset Statement 6:

"People are either born with it or not, and I'm not."

Your Growth Mindset Response:

____

____

____

Section 3: Handling Failure and Criticism

Fixed Mindset Statement 7:

"There's no point in trying if I might fail."

Your Growth Mindset Response:

____

____

____

Fixed Mindset Statement 8:

"When I receive criticism, it means I'm a failure."

Your Growth Mindset Response:

____

____

____

Fixed Mindset Statement 9:

"If I don't succeed quickly, it means I never will."

Your Growth Mindset Response:

___

___

___

Reflect on how rephrasing these thoughts can influence your actions and mindset going forward. Which of these reframed responses do you find most challenging, and why? What can you do to more consistently apply a growth mindset in your daily life?

FINAL THOUGHTS

In this chapter, we explored the powerful concept of a growth mindset, a crucial tool for personal development and academic success, especially for us as teens facing today's challenges. Originally introduced by psychologist Carol Dweck, the idea separates our views on abilities and intelligence into two categories: fixed and growth mindsets. If you have a fixed mindset, you might think your skills and intelligence are set and unchangeable, which can make you shy away from challenges and give up easily. But with a growth mindset, you believe you can develop and improve these abilities through effort and persistence.

We learned that having a fixed mindset might stop us from trying new things because we fear failure and criticism. It can make us think effort is pointless if we're not immediately good at something, leading to frustration and a lack of fulfillment. On the flip side, adopting a growth mindset means seeing effort as a path to mastering new skills, feeling inspired by others' successes, and viewing challenges as chances to grow stronger and smarter.

Throughout the chapter, we discovered practical ways to cultivate a growth mindset. First, it's about recognizing those moments when we slip into fixed mindset thinking—like when we tell ourselves we're just not good at something and never will be. Changing these thoughts involves embracing challenges and seeing them as opportunities to learn rather than obstacles.

We also talked about the importance of not fearing failure. Instead of seeing it as a setback, it's more helpful to view failure as a lesson and a normal part of learning and growing. Valuing effort over perfection helps us focus on the process of learning, which is where real improvement happens. Staying open to continuous learning and persistent effort teaches us that improvement is always possible.

Dealing with criticism effectively is another key skill we covered. Instead of reacting defensively to feedback, taking a moment to process and learn from it can turn criticism into a valuable tool for growth. We learned not to take things personally and to see feedback as a means to better ourselves, not as a judgment of our worth.

The role of our environment also plays a part in shaping our mindset. Surrounding ourselves with people who also embrace growth and learning can really boost our own efforts. Celebrating not just our own achievements but also those of our peers fosters a supportive community that values progress and effort.

To wrap this final chapter up, embracing a growth mindset isn't just about improving our grades or skills—it's about setting ourselves up for a fulfilling life. It teaches us to see opportunities where others see limitations and encourages us to keep pushing ourselves, no matter the challenges. By understanding and applying the principles of a growth mindset, we can navigate school and life more effectively, achieving not just academic success but also personal growth and satisfaction.

In the next chapter, we will summarize this book and tie it all together to optimize the ways it can benefit your life.

Conclusion

As we wrap up our journey, it's important to revisit the core message and insights this book has offered. This is not merely a recap of the content but a consolidation of its essence, aimed at empowering you, the reader, with a renewed perspective on self-acceptance, self-worth, and the power of personal transformation.

First and foremost, remember that the insecurities and fears you face are common experiences for many teens. You are not alone in your struggles, and these challenges do not define your worth or capabilities. Instead, they are stepping stones, each offering a unique opportunity for growth and learning. This book has been your guide, providing tools and strategies to navigate these challenges, but the true transformation begins with you—when you choose to embrace yourself with compassion, courage, and grace.

Throughout these pages, we've delved into various aspects of building a positive self-image. From understanding the impact of social media on our self-perception to learning practical steps for enhancing self-confidence, each chapter was designed to equip you with knowledge and tools to foster a healthier relationship with yourself. The key takeaway is that your value does not depend on external validation or comparison with others. Your worth is intrinsic, and recognizing this is the first step toward living a more fulfilling life.

Self-love is an essential foundation for all other forms of success and happiness. It influences how you see yourself and how you interact with the world. When you operate from a place of self-love, you make choices that align with your best interests and reflect your true self. This alignment brings about a profound sense of peace and satisfaction, as you are no longer swayed by the fleeting opinions of others.

Self-confidence, on the other hand, is about trusting your abilities and believing in your potential to achieve your goals. This book has shown you that confidence can be built through experiences of success, as well as through the challenges that you overcome. Each success story shared in these pages, from overcoming public speaking fears to thriving after personal setbacks, serves as a testament to the resilience and strength that you too possess.

Now, as you turn the last page of this book, it's time to translate these insights into action. Start small, with daily affirmations that reinforce your self-worth. Set achievable goals that challenge you and allow you to experience success. Surround yourself with supportive people who uplift you and reflect the values you aspire to embody. Remember, the growth of your self-esteem is a continuous journey that requires patience, persistence, and a positive mindset.

Let the stories of those who have walked this path before you be your inspiration. For instance, consider the story of Emma, a teen who transformed her self-doubt into self-empowerment by applying the principles discussed in this book. Emma used to shy away from challenges, fearing failure and rejection. However, by practicing self-compassion and stepping out of her comfort zone, she began to see herself in a new light. Her journey from insecurity to confidence is a powerful example of how adopting a proactive approach to personal development can lead to remarkable changes in how one feels and lives.

As you move forward, keep in mind that the ultimate success is not about reaching a destination but about embracing the process of becoming more authentically you. Every step you take towards understanding and loving yourself contributes to a stronger, more resilient you. This is how you build a life not defined by fear or doubt but powered by confidence and self-love.

And so, with the tools and knowledge you now hold, step into your power. Nurture your self-esteem, embrace your unique journey, and shape your future with intention and joy. You have the power to transform your life—one positive, self-affirming decision at a time.

Lastly, if this book has touched your life, if it has given you insights or tools that have made a difference, consider sharing your experience. Write a review, share it with friends, or simply pass on the lessons you've learned. Your feedback is invaluable, helping others discover this resource and, potentially, transforming their lives as well.

Thank you for allowing this book into your life. Remember, you are worthy, just as you are. Your uniqueness is your superpower, and your potential knows no bounds. Go forth with courage and confidence, for the path ahead is yours to shape.

Keeping the Game Alive

Now that you have everything you need to overcome insecurities, conquer fear, and embrace mindfulness to build a positive self-image, it's time to pass on your newfound knowledge and show other readers where they can find the same help.

Simply by leaving your honest opinion of this book on Amazon, you'll show other teen girls where they can find the information they're looking for, and pass their passion for self-love, self-confidence, and self-esteem forward.

Thank you for your help. Self-love and confidence are kept alive when we pass on our knowledge – and you're helping me to do just that.

Scan the QR code to leave your review on Amazon.

References

7 ways to help your teen strengthen their friendships. (2024, March 26). Friendships. https://parents.au.reachout.com/friendships-and-dating/friendships/help-your-teenager-make-great-friends

90 Inspiring Growth Mindset Quotes for Kids. (2024, May 21). Mental Health Center Kids. https://mentalhealthcenterkids.com/blogs/articles/growth-mindset-quotes

A guide to conflict resolution for Teens. (2023, November 21). Mental Health Center Kids. https://mentalhealthcenterkids.com/blogs/articles/conflict-resolution-for-teens

Abu-Atta, S. (2023, January 11). *My Story with the Mindsets*. https://www.linkedin.com/pulse/my-story-mindsets-sujud-abu-atta/

Alcamo, K. (2017, June 13). *Unhealthy Friendships in Adolescence: How to know when to let go - GoodTherapy.org therapy blog*. GoodTherapy.org Therapy Blog. https://www.goodtherapy.org/blog/unhealthy-friendships-in-adolescence-how-to-know-when-to-let-go-0614175/

All-or-Nothing Thinking: 3 Ways to Stop Throwing in the Towel. (n.d.). https://www.betterup.com/blog/all-or-nothing-thinking

And have confidence in yourself and your abilities! (n.d.). https://www.brainyquote.com/quotes/kirstin_maldonado_985687?src=t_surround_yourself

APA PsycNet. (n.d.). https://psycnet.apa.org/record/2017-57603-001

Ascend Healthcare. (2023, June 28). *Assessing a teen's social confidence*. https://www.ascendhc.com/teen-rehab-blog/assessing-a-teens-social-confidence/

Becker, J. (n.d.). *How to Stop Comparing Yourself to others - a helpful guide*. Becomingminimalist. https://www.becomingminimalist.com/compare-less/

Being, G. (2023a, April 11). *How does self awareness help boost your confidence?* Grace Being. https://grace-being.com/emotional-intelligence/how-does-self-awareness-help-boost-your-confidence/

Being, G. (2023b, April 11). *How does self awareness help boost your confidence?* Grace Being. https://grace-being.com/emotional-intelligence/how-does-self-awareness-help-boost-your-confidence/

Bennett, T. (2023, October 20). *People-pleasing: A breakdown of the bad habit and how to kick it*. Thriveworks. https://thriveworks.com/help-with/self-improvement/people-pleasing

BetterHelp Editorial Team. (2024, May 2). *How Perfectionism can Harm your self esteem | BetterHelp*. https://www.betterhelp.com/advice/general/how-perfectionism-can-harm-your-self-esteem/

biglifejournal.com. (n.d.). *Fixed Mindset vs. Growth Mindset Examples*. Big Life Journal. https://biglifejournal.com/blogs/blog/fixed-mindset-vs-growth-mindset-examples

Bilanich, B., & Bilanich, B. (2012, July 12). *Surround yourself with positive people | Bud Bilanich*. Bud Bilanich | Your Career Mentor. https://budbilanich.com/surround-yourself-with-positive-people/

Bluth, K. (2024, January 23). *How Self-Compassion can Improve Teen Mental Health*. Mindful. https://www.mindful.org/how-self-compassion-can-improve-teen-mental-health

Body image in childhood. (n.d.). Mental Health Foundation. https://www.mentalhealth.org.uk/explore-mental-health/articles/body-image-report-executive-summary/body-image-childhood

Bradbury, Z. (2021, November 4). *How to stop comparing your body to others*. Butterfly Foundation. https://butterfly.org.au/stop-comparing-your-body-to-others/

Braime, H. (2020, November 14). *Why There's no such thing as "Unhealthy" emotions*. Possibility Change. https://possibilitychange.com/unhealthy-emotions/

Calm Editorial Team. (2024a, February 6). *5 simple ways to practice mindfulness in daily life — Calm Blog*. Calm Blog. https://www.calm.com/blog/5-simple-ways-to-practice-mindfulness-in-daily-life

Calm Editorial Team. (2024b, February 8). *How to *actually* practice self-compassion? Try these 5 exercises — Calm Blog*. Calm Blog. https://www.calm.com/blog/how-to-practice-self-compassion

Calm Editorial Team. (2024c, February 13). *How to improve self-esteem in 7 steps using mindfulness — Calm Blog*. Calm Blog. https://www.calm.com/blog/how-to-improve-your-self-esteem-with-mindfulness

Capecchi, S., & Saleh, N. (n.d.). *Mindfulness for Teens: How it works, benefits, & 11 Exercises to try*. Choosing Therapy. https://www.choosingtherapy.com/mindfulness-for-teens/

Capecchi, S., & Saleh, N. (2022, June 8). *Mindfulness for Teens: How it works, benefits, & 11 Exercises to try*. Choosing Therapy. https://www.choosingtherapy.com/mindfulness-for-teens/

Confidence in pre-teens and teenagers. (2021, November 5). Raising Children Network. https://raisingchildren.net.au/pre-teens/development/social-emotional-development/confidence-in-teens

Cordeiro, M. R. D. (n.d.). *Body image issues affect many, adolescent girls and adult women especially – Ocean State Stories*. https://oceanstatestories.org/body-image-issues-affect-many-adolescent-girls-and-adult-women-especially/

Cpt, S. C. (2022, September 7). *The benefits of Self-Compassion*. Psych Central.

https://psychcentral.com/blog/practicing-self-compassion-when-you-have-a-mental-illness

Cuncic, A., MA. (2023, February 13). *How to stop negative thoughts*. Verywell Mind. https://www.verywellmind.com/how-to-change-negative-thinking-3024843

Davis, T. (2021, January 13). *6 Science based Self-Compassion exercises*. Psychology Today. https://www.psychologytoday.com/us/blog/click-here-happiness/202101/6-science-based-self-compassion-exercises

DeGroff, E. (2020, September 22). *Great Quotes for Kids about Feelings and Emotions*. InspireMyKids. https://inspiremykids.com/14388/

Disqualifying the positive: how to overcome it. (2024, January 12). Mental Health Center Kids. https://mentalhealthcenterkids.com/blogs/articles/disqualifying-the-positive

Dowches-Wheeler, J. (2021a, October 25). *How Self-Awareness Builds Confidence — Bright Space Coaching | Stress Management & Lifestyle Medicine*. Bright Space Coaching | Stress Management & Lifestyle Medicine. https://www.brightspacecoaching.com/blog/2018/6/20/how-self-awareness-builds-confidence

Dowches-Wheeler, J. (2021b, October 25). *How Self-Awareness Builds Confidence — Bright Space Coaching | Stress Management & Lifestyle Medicine*. Bright Space Coaching | Stress Management & Lifestyle Medicine. https://www.brightspacecoaching.com/blog/2018/6/20/how-self-awareness-builds-confidence

Emotion regulation. (n.d.). Pschology Today. https://www.psychologytoday.com/us/basics/emotion-regulation

Emotional reasoning: a cognitive distortion. (2024, January 12). Mental Health Center Kids. https://mentalhealthcenterkids.com/blogs/articles/emotional-reasoning

Five deep breathing exercises for kids and teens. (n.d.). Cedars-Sinai. https://www.cedars-sinai.org/blog/five-deep-breathing-exercises-for-kids-and-teens.html

Fleming, W. (2023, July 13). *Six Boundaries for Teens They'll Thank You For Later*. parentingteensandtweens.com. https://parentingteensandtweens.com/boundaries-for-teens/

'Frenemies' and toxic friendships: pre-teens and teenagers. (2024, March 7). Raising Children Network. https://raisingchildren.net.au/pre-teens/behaviour/peers-friends-trends/frenemies

Friedman, D. (2024, March 20). *The Ultimate Guide To Journaling For Teenagers (w/ Resources)*. Modern Teen. https://modernteen.co/journaling-for-teenagers/

Friends and friendships: pre-teens and teenagers. (2024, March 12). Raising Children Network. https://raisingchildren.net.au/pre-teens/behaviour/peers-friends-trends/teen-friendships

Friends forever? How to deal with a toxic friendship. (2023, February 16). Kids Help Phone. https://kidshelpphone.ca/get-info/friends-forever-how-deal-toxic-friendship/

Galperin, S. (2022, February 11). *Social anxiety in Teens: How to overcome your social anxiety*. CBT Psychology. https://cbtpsychology.com/socialanxiety/

Golan, M. (2015). Gender differences in respect to Self-Esteem and body image as well as response to adolescents' School-Based Prevention programs. *Journal of Psychology & Clinical Psychiatry, 2*(5). https://doi.org/10.15406/jpcpy.2015.02.00092

Gomez, T., Quinones-Camacho, L., & Davis, E. (n.d.). *Building a Sense of Self: The Link between Emotion Regulation and Self-Esteem in Young Adults*. Escholarship. https://escholarship.org/content/qt8db0d25w/qt8db0d25w_noSplash_121fa3692ec22ae97e8c25fb274f5ffe.pdf

Goodman, E., PhD. (2023, April 29). *Playing with Fear: How Changing Your Mindset Can Change Your Life*. https://www.linkedin.com/pulse/playing-fear-how-changing-your-mindset-can-change-eric-goodman-ph-d-/

GoodTherapy Editor Team. (2019, June 17). *Self–Compassion*. https://www.goodtherapy.org/learn-about-therapy/issues/self-compassion

Gordon, S. (2021, July 26). *What teens need to know about boundaries*. Verywell Family. https://www.verywellfamily.com/boundaries-what-every-teen-needs-to-know-5119428

Gordon, S. (2022, March 31). *Frenemy or friend? How to spot the signs of unhealthy friendship in kids*. Verywell Family. https://www.verywellfamily.com/how-to-spot-the-signs-of-an-unhealthy-friendship-5223470

Gough, K. J. (2022, June 15). *Why Perfectionism in Girls is so Pervasive and How to Change It*. Metro Parent. https://www.metroparent.com/parenting/tweens-teens/why-perfectionism-in-girls-is-so-pervasive-and-how-to-change-it/

Grimste, M. (2023, March 29). *Toxic vs Healthy Friendships | What's the Difference for Teenagers? — Mallory Grimste, LCSW - Mental Health Therapist for Teens and Young Adults*. Mallory Grimste, LCSW - Mental Health Therapist for Teens and Young Adults. https://www.mallorygrimste.com/counseling-blog/toxicvshealthyfriendships

HappierTherapy. (2024, April 9). *I-Statement Worksheet for Youth | HappierTHERAPY*. HappierTherapy. https://happiertherapy.com/i-statement-worksheet-for-youth/

Hartney, E. (2023, November 8). *10 Cognitive Distortions That Can Cause Negative Thinking*. VeryWellmind. https://www.verywellmind.com/ten-cognitive-distortions-identified-in-cbt-22412#:

Harvard Health. (2021, February 12). *4 ways to boost your self-compassion*. https://www.health.harvard.edu/mental-health/4-ways-to-boost-your-self-compassion

Haupt, A. (2024, May 21). *Self-Compassion: what it is and how to get better at it*.

EverydayHealth.com. https://www.everydayhealth.com/emotional-health/tips-for-showing-yourself-some-self-compassion/

How can I improve my self-esteem. (n.d.). Nemours TeensHealth. https://kidshealth.org/en/teens/self-esteem.html

How to handle peer pressure. (n.d.). Fairfax County Public Schools. https://www.fcps.edu/student-wellness-tips/peer-pressure

How to help children Stop comparing themselves to others - Shiminly. (2022, August 2). Shiminly. https://shiminly.com/how-to-help-children-stop-comparing-themselves-to-others/

How to Practice Self-Love - Headspace. (n.d.). Headspace. https://www.headspace.com/mindfulness/self-love

Hughes, B. (2023, March 10). *The relationship between perfectionist thinking and body image.* Authentically Be You Counseling & Wellness Studio. https://www.authenticallybeyou.com/blog/the-relationship-between-perfectionist-thinking-and-body-image

Hutchinson, T. (2022, September 7). *Self-Compassion: The Benefits to Your Mental Health - Tracy Hutchinson, PhD | Fort Myers Therapy.* Tracy Hutchinson, PhD | Fort Myers Therapy. https://www.drtracyhutchinson.com/benefits-to-self-compassion-benefits-to-your-mental-health/

Huziej, M. (2023, December 19). *All about Magnification and Minimisation.* CPD Online College. https://cpdonline.co.uk/knowledge-base/mental-health/magnification-and-minimisation/#how-to-overcome-magnification-and-minimisation

I (14F) am insecure about my looks! (n.d.). https://www.reddit.com/r/TwoXChromosomes/comments/9cvog3/i_14f_am_insecure_about_my_looks/

INHERVISION. (2018). *How to Stop People-Pleasing & Start Finding Happiness within.* https://inhervision.com/wp-content/uploads/2018/12/How-to-stop-people-pleasing-worksheet-1.pdf

Jax, N. (n.d.). *Your uniqueness is what makes you special, and that is beautiful.* Brainy Quotes. https://www.brainyquote.com/quotes/nia_jax_963854?src=t_uniqueness

Jiotsa, B., Naccache, B., Duval, M., Rocher, B., & Grall-Bronnec, M. (2021). Social media use and body image disorders: association between frequency of comparing one's own physical appearance to that of people being followed on social media And body dissatisfaction And drive for thinness. *National Library of Medicine.* https://www.ncbi.nlm.nih.gov/pmc/articles/PMC8001450/

Jodie, & Jodie. (2023, February 21). *How your mindset affects outcomes - Dr Jodie.* Dr Jodie. https://drjodie.com.au/how-your-mindset-affects-outcomes/

Johann. (2023, September 24). Embracing flaws and quirks: The beauty of imperfection. *Medium.* https://medium.com/@johann-a/embracing-flaws-and-quirks-the-beauty-of-imperfection-ab8b14eb72b9

Kika. (2024, April 18). *Beauty comes in many colors, shapes and sizes.* A Life in Progress. https://www.alifeinprogress.ca/beauty-comes-colors-shapes-sizes/

LaCroix, M. A. (2023, February 10). *What causes People-Pleasing, and how to break the cycle.* The Hearty Fig. https://www.theheartyfig.com/blog/what-causes-people-pleasing

Lagidze, N. (2024, March 9). *8 people-pleasing behaviors stemming from a lack of self-esteem.* Hack Spirit. https://hackspirit.com/people-pleasing-behaviors-stemming-from-a-lack-of-self-esteem/

Lahm, M. (2022, September 10). *How to make friends as a teenager.* The Teen Mag. https://www.theteenmagazine.com/how-to-make-new-friends-as-a-teenager

Lcsw, S. M. (2015, December 8). *What causes perfectionism?* Psych Central. https://psychcentral.com/blog/imperfect/2015/12/what-causes-perfectionism#1

Lebow, H. I. (2021a, July 20). *18 tips to Stop being a People-Pleaser.* Psych Central. https://psychcentral.com/health/tips-to-stop-being-a-people-pleaser#traits-of-people-pleasers

Lebow, H. I. (2021b, July 20). *18 tips to Stop being a People-Pleaser.* Psych Central. https://psychcentral.com/health/tips-to-stop-being-a-people-pleaser#traits-of-people-pleasers

Lebow, H. I. (2022, April 6). *Do you know how to manage your emotions and why it matters?* Psych Central. https://psychcentral.com/health/emotional-regulation

Lindsay. (2023, September 25). *How to Stop comparing your body to others - 5 tips | OutshiningED.* OutshiningED. https://www.outshininged.com/blog-post/body-comparison/

Lpc, H. T. M. (2021, October 26). *Overcoming the mental filter (A cognitive distortion) -.* https://courageousandmindful.com/overcoming-the-mental-filter-a-cognitive-distortion/

Lubag, S. C. (2024, February 25). Selfie culture and self-esteem: Study unravels the impact of social media on adolescent girls. *PsyPost - Psychology News.* https://www.psypost.org/selfie-culture-and-self-esteem-study-unravels-the-impact-of-social-media-on-adolescent-girls/

Mba, C. M. P. (2024, March 15). *How to Practice Self-Compassion: 8 Techniques and tips.* PositivePsychology.com. https://positivepsychology.com/how-to-practice-self-compassion/

McComb, S. E., & Mills, J. S. (2021). Young women's body image following upwards comparison to Instagram models: The role of physical appearance perfectionism and cognitive emotion regulation. *Body Image, 38,* 49–62. https://doi.org/10.1016/j.bodyim.2021.03.012

Middleearthnj. (2011, January 10). *How teens can be and pick a good friend.* Middle

Earth. https://middleearthnj.org/2011/01/10/how-teens-can-be-and-pick-a-good-friend/

Middleearthnj. (2019, November 18). *How to combat Perfectionism in Teens.* Middle Earth. https://middleearthnj.org/2019/10/14/how-to-combat-perfectionism-in-teens/

Mindful Eating – Center for Young Women's Health. (n.d.). https://youngwomenshealth.org/guides/mindful-eating/

Mindfulness. (n.d.). Nemours TeenHealth. https://kidshealth.org/en/teens/mindfulness.html

Mindfulness can Increase Self-Confidence | HealthyPlace. (2013, March 13). https://www.healthyplace.com/blogs/buildingselfesteem/2013/03/how-mindfulness-can-increase-self-confidence

Neff, K. (2009). The role of Self-Compassion in Development: A Healthier Way to Relate to oneself. *National Library of Medicine.* https://www.ncbi.nlm.nih.gov/pmc/articles/PMC2790748/

Neff, K., & Germer, C. (2022, October 19). *The Transformative effects of Mindful Self-Compassion.* Mindful. https://www.mindful.org/the-transformative-effects-of-mindful-self-compassion/

Nunez, K. (2020, August 10). *The benefits of progressive muscle relaxation and how to do it.* Healthline. https://www.healthline.com/health/progressive-muscle-relaxation#how-to-do-it

Oglesby, A. (2024, April 3). *How to Make Friends Easily if You're a Teen (with Pictures).* wikiHow. https://www.wikihow.com/Make-Friends-Easily-if-You%27re-a-Teen

Our Mindful Life. (2022, January 17). *39 Perfectionism quotes to love the perfectly imperfect you.* https://www.ourmindfullife.com/perfectionism-quotes/

Pedersen, T. (2023, February 27). *How does social media affect body image?* Psych Central. https://psychcentral.com/health/how-the-media-affects-body-image

Peer pressure. (n.d.). Nemours TeensHealth. https://kidshealth.org/en/teens/peer-pressure.html

Peetz, C. (2023, November 9). The State of Girls' Mental Health and Self-Confidence, in charts. *Education Week.* https://www.edweek.org/leadership/the-state-of-girls-mental-health-and-self-confidence-in-charts/2023/11

Perfectionism and Self-Worth. (n.d.). EMPOWER COUNSELING & CONSULTING OF ATLANTA. https://www.empowercca.com/mental-health-blog/perfectionism-and-self-worth

Perfectionism in children and teens. (n.d.). https://www.sedonasky.org/blog/perfectionism-in-children-and-teens

Persona. (2024, April 8). *What is a growth mindset and how to develop it in 9 steps.* Persona. https://www.personatalent.com/development/how-to-cultivate-a-growth-mindset

Personalization: a common cognitive distortion. (2024, January 28). Mental Health Center Kids. https://mentalhealthcenterkids.com/blogs/articles/personalization-cognitive-distortion

Peterson, T., & Bass, P., III. (2023, November 29). *Meditation: Benefits, How It Works, & Exercises to Try*. Choosing Theraoy. https://www.choosingtherapy.com/meditation/

Pikiewicz, K. (2021a, December 1). *The Power of Self-Awareness for Teens - Digging deep*. Digging Deep. https://diggingdeep.org/power-self-awareness-teens/

Pikiewicz, K. (2021b, December 1). *The Power of Self-Awareness for Teens - Digging deep*. Digging Deep. https://diggingdeep.org/power-self-awareness-teens/

Pontz, E. (2021, March 31). *Strategies to handle peer pressure*. Center for Parent and Teen Communication. https://parentandteen.com/handle-peer-pressure/

Psychology Everywhere. (2022, March 9). *How low self-esteem can affect your teenager - Psychology Everywhere*. https://psychologyeverywhere.com/articles/how-low-self-esteem-can-affect-your-teenager/

PsyD, D. N., & PsyD, D. N. (2023, March 23). *Teenage Friendships: Why they are so important and how to address common issues*. Simi Psychological Group. https://simipsychologicalgroup.com/teenage-friendships-why-are-they-so-important

Puharich, R. (2022, February 27). Growth Mindset for Teens - TeenLearner. *TeenLearner*. https://teenlearner.com/growth-mindset-for-teens/

Samson, J. (2021, December 7). 7 Best tips on how to overcome Labeling - Judith Samson - Medium. *Medium*. https://medium.com/@judygichobi/7-best-tips-on-how-to-overcome-labeling-b8f634c81d44

School Counseling Success. (2019). *Building resiliency and reducing anxiety by overcoming perfectionism*. https://positivekids.ca/wp-content/uploads/2021/01/BuildingResiliencyandReducingAnxietybyOVERCOMINGPERFECTIONISM lessonplan-1-1.pdf

Scripps Health. (2024, May 1). How does peer pressure affect a teen's social development? *Scripps Health*. https://www.scripps.org/news_items/4648-how-does-peer-pressure-affect-a-teen-s-social-development

Self awareness and self esteem. (n.d.). https://more-selfesteem.com/more-self-esteem/building-self-esteem/what-is-self-esteem/self-awareness-and-self-esteem/

Self confidence in teens. (2024, March 26). https://parents.au.reachout.com/self-esteem-body-image/self-confidence/self-confidence-and-teenagers

Self-Awareness: What is it & how to develop it. (n.d.-a). https://www.betterup.com/blog/what-is-self-awareness

Self-Awareness: What is it & how to develop it. (n.d.-b). https://www.betterup.com/blog/what-is-self-awareness

Self-Compassion. (2024, May 24). *Self-Compassion by Kristin Neff: Join the community now*. https://self-compassion.org/

Self-compassion for pre-teens and teenagers. (2023a, October 18). Raising Children Network. https://raisingchildren.net.au/teens/mental-health-physical-health/about-mental-health/self-compassion-teenagers

Self-compassion for pre-teens and teenagers. (2023b, October 18). Raising Children Network. https://raisingchildren.net.au/teens/mental-health-physical-health/about-mental-health/self-compassion-teenagers

Setting healthy boundaries for teens. (2023, December 15). Mental Health Center Kids. https://mentalhealthcenterkids.com/blogs/articles/boundaries-for-teens

Should statements: How to reframe the way you think. (2024, January 12). Mental Health Center Kids. https://mentalhealthcenterkids.com/blogs/articles/should-statements

Signs of Low Self-Esteem in Children & Teens. (n.d.). HealthyChildren.org. https://www.healthychildren.org/English/ages-stages/gradeschool/Pages/Signs-of-Low-Self-Esteem.aspx

Simeon, D. (2020, October 1). *Teens benefit from a growth mindset, (Hard work matters)*. Your Teen Magazine. https://yourteenmag.com/family-life/communication/growth-mindset-work-hard

Smith, M. M., Sherry, S. B., Chen, S., Saklofske, D. H., Mushquash, C., Flett, G. L., & Hewitt, P. L. (2017). The perniciousness of perfectionism: A meta-analytic review of the perfectionism–suicide relationship. *Journal of Personality, 86*(3), 522–542. https://doi.org/10.1111/jopy.12333

Smith, M. M., Sherry, S. B., Rnic, K., Saklofske, D. H., Enns, M., & Gralnick, T. (2016). Are Perfectionism Dimensions Vulnerability Factors for Depressive Symptoms after Controlling for Neuroticism? A Meta–analysis of 10 Longitudinal Studies. *European Journal of Personality, 30*(2), 201–212. https://doi.org/10.1002/per.2053

Smith, T. (2023, February 21). *57 People Pleaser quotes: Stop trying to make people happy*. Happier Human. https://www.happierhuman.com/people-pleaser-quotes/

Spokane, I. (2023a, August 30). *5 Self-Awareness activities for adolescents*. Imagine Spokane. https://www.spokaneimagine.com/mental-health-blog/5-self-awareness-activities-for-adolescents/

Spokane, I. (2023b, August 30). *5 Self-Awareness activities for adolescents*. Imagine Spokane. https://www.spokaneimagine.com/mental-health-blog/5-self-awareness-activities-for-adolescents/

Stelle. (2023, December 22). *Fit and Active: 12 Great Workout Routines for Teenage Girls*. https://stelleworld.com/blogs/news/workout-routines-for-teenage-girls

Stop overgeneralisation to build Self-Esteem | HealthyPlace. (2015, December 1). https://

www.healthyplace.com/blogs/buildingselfesteem/2015/12/stop-overgeneralisation-to-build-self-esteem

Stuck, A., & Sookdeo, T. (2023, October 31). *Emotional Regulation: Skills to Help Regulate Your Emotions*. Choosing Therapy. https://www.choosingtherapy.com/emotional-regulation/

Sunflower Empowerment. (2023, October 3). *How a growth mindset can increase confidence and reduce anxiety*. Counselling Directory. https://www.counselling-directory.org.uk/memberarticles/how-a-growth-mindset-can-increase-confidence-and-reduce-anxiety

Tallon, M., & Tallon, M. (2020, May 11). *10 simple ways to practice mindfulness in our daily life*. Monique Tallon. https://moniquetallon.com/10-simple-ways-to-practice-mindfulness-in-our-daily-life/

Team, E. S. (2024, March 22). Effective guide to Conflict Resolution for Teenagers. *ESS Global Training Solutions*. https://esoftskills.com/conflict-resolution-for-teens/#Peer_Mediation_in_Conflict_Resolution_in_Schools

Teens and Peer Pressure - Children's health. (n.d.). https://www.childrens.com/health-wellness/helping-teens-deal-with-peer-pressure

The Magic of "Mindset" — Sparkle stories. (n.d.). Sparkle Stories. https://www.sparklestories.com/blog/post/magic-of-mindset/

Therapy worksheets, tools, and handouts | Therapist Aid. (n.d.). Therapist Aid. https://www.therapistaid.com/

Timpangburn. (2021, May 11). *Less than spectacular: overcoming insecurity through a growth mindset – Tim Pangburn*. https://www.timpangburn.com/2021/05/11/less-than-spectacular-overcoming-insecurity-through-a-growth-mindset/

Tri-MED Health & Wellness & By Tri-MED Health & Wellness. (2022, June 9). 5 Ways to Embrace Your Flaws and Rewrite Your Life - Tri-MED Integrative Psychiatry & Sleep Medicine. *Tri-MED Integrative Psychiatry & Sleep Medicine*. https://www.trimedhealth.com/5-ways-embrace-flaws-rewrite-your-life/

Trzesniewski, K., Donnellan, B., Moffitt, T., & Robins, R. (2006, March). *Low Self-Esteem during adolescence predicts poor health, criminal behavior, and limited economic prospects during adulthood*. ResearchGate. https://www.researchgate.net/publication/7210504_Low_Self-Esteem_During_Adolescence_Predicts_Poor_Health_Criminal_Behavior_and_Limited_Economic_Prospects_during_Adulthood https://www.psychologytoday.com/us/blog/shyness-is-nice/201809/why-self-confidence-is-more-important-you-think

U, F. (2017, July 25). How to tell your real friends from your fake ones before heading to college. *Teen Vogue*. https://www.teenvogue.com/story/how-to-tell-your-real-friends-from-your-fake-ones-before-heading-to-college/

UNIPOLAR DEPRESSION. (n.d.). *Negative Thoughts Trigger Negative Feelings*, 333–

337. https://counselinghuntsville.com/wp-content/uploads/2020/07/Negative-Thoughts-Trigger-Negative-Feelings.pdf

UNIVERSITY OF CALIFORNIA SAN FRANCISCO Langley Porter Psychiatric Hospital & Clinics. (n.d.). REHABILITATION SERVICES PATIENT EDUCATION MANUAL emotion regulation skills. In *UNIVERSITY OF CALIFORNIA SAN FRANCISCO Langley Porter Psychiatric Hospital & Clinics* (Vol. 2). https://psychiatry.ucsf.edu/sites/psych.ucsf.edu/files/EMOTION%20REGULATION%20SKILLS%20MANUAL.pdf

Unknown, U. (n.d.). *15-Minute Mindfulness Body Scan Script for Teens*. https://www.mindfulschools.org/wp/wp-content/uploads/2019/02/Practice-Script-for-Teens-Body-Scan.pdf

Vacca, M., Ballesio, A., & Lombardo, C. (2020). The relationship between perfectionism and eating-related symptoms in adolescents: A systematic review. *European Eating Disorders Review, 29*(1), 32–51. https://doi.org/10.1002/erv.2793

Vallejo, M. (2022, September 5). How to avoid jumping to conclusions: 4 Effective tools. *Blunt Therapy*. https://www.blunt-therapy.com/jumping-to-conclusions/

Van Der Zande Kidpower Founder and Executive Director, I. (2022a, August 18). *Teen consent and boundary skills*. Kidpower International. https://www.kidpower.org/library/article/teen-boundaries/

Van Der Zande Kidpower Founder and Executive Director, I. (2022b, August 18). *Teen consent and boundary skills*. Kidpower International. https://www.kidpower.org/library/article/teen-boundaries/

Van Edwards, V. (2023, October 30). *11 expert tips to Stop being a people pleaser and start doing you*. Science of People. https://www.scienceofpeople.com/people-pleaser/

Weis, C. (2022, September 25). *7 Benefits of Promoting a growth mindset in students*. For the Love of Teachers. https://www.fortheloveofteachers.com/7-benefits-of-promoting-a-growth-mindset-in-students/

What is a people pleaser? (2024, February 25). WebMD. https://www.webmd.com/mental-health/what-is-a-people-pleaser

Made in the USA
Columbia, SC
15 June 2025

59425330R00120